The Encyclopedia of CARS

VOLUME FOUR – Humber to Maserati

The Encyclopedia of CARS

VOLUME FOUR – Humber to Maserati

Chelsea House Publishers

Philadelphia

Edited by Chris Horton
Foreword by Karl Ludvigsen

Published in 1998 by
Chelsea House Publishers
1974 Sproul Road, Suite 400
P.O. Box 914
Broomall, PA 19008-0914

**Copyright © 1998 Regency House
Publishing Limited**

Printed in Italy

**Library of Congress Cataloging-in-Publication
Data**
Encyclopedia of Cars/edited by Chris Horton:
foreword by Karl Ludvigsen.
     p.   cm.
    Includes indexes.
    ISBN 0-7910-4865-9 (vol. 1)
    ISBN 0-7910-4866-7 (vol. 2)
    ISBN 0-7910-4867-5 (vol. 3)
    ISBN 0-7910-4868-3 (vol. 4)
    ISBN 0-7910-4869-1 (vol. 5)
    ISBN 0-7910-4870-5 (vol. 6)
    ISBN 0-7910-4871-3 (vol. 7)
    ISBN 0-7910-4864-0 (set)

1. Automobiles–Encyclopedias. I. Horton, Chris.
TL9. E5233 1997   97-17890
629.222 03–DC21   CIP

Page 2: Lexus GS300 Sport
Page 3: Maserati Biturbo
Right: Jaguar XK8

Contents

A 1933 Humber 'Twelve'

Humber

Great Britain
1899–1976

Humber was one of the oldest companies in the British motor industry. First established by Thomas Humber in 1867, the firm originally built bicycles.

After being involved with the production of the three-wheeled Pennington, Humber produced its first car – a single-cylinder, 3½hp model, which appeared in 1899. In the very early days Humber experimented with front-wheel-drive, and produced both three- and four-wheeled cars.

The company built motorized tricycles until 1905, as well as a voiturette and a more successful De Dion-engined 4½hp car with shaft-drive from 1901. In the following two years Humber built four-cylinder 12hp and 20hp models, and a three-cylinder machine with mechanically operated inlet valves instead of the earlier suction-activated valves.

One of the most famous cars of its time was the 1903 Humberette. This was shaft-driven via a two-speed gearbox and powered by a 600cc engine of De Dion design. The car was uprated in 1904.

.P. HUMBER
Seater Car

Above: 6½hp Royal Humberette, c. 1904
Left: 1913 10hp Humber two-seater

Humbers were produced at two factories until 1908 – at Beeston, Nottinghamshire, and at Coventry, Warwickshire; the Coventry Humbers were cheaper models.

A wide range of cars was produced by

Below: From the earliest days of the motor industry, Humber built an interesting range of cars, both three- and four-wheelers, and experimented with front-wheel-drive. However models like this 8hp Humber, of 1909, were more conventional.

Humber before World War I, from an 8hp to a 6.3-litre model. From 1912 the new Humberette cyclecar was available with an air-cooled 998cc engine. After the war Humber concentrated on building reliable family cars, using inlet-over-exhaust-valve cylinder-head configurations from 1923.

Above: 1923 Humber 8/18hp Chummy Car
Below: 1929 Humber saloon

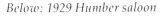

Humber acquired commercial-vehicle manufacturers Commer Cars Ltd. in 1926, and took Hillman under its wing in 1928. By this time Humber had introduced an 1100cc 9/20 model, a two-litre 14/40 and a larger, six-cylinder 20/55.

Six-cylinder models introduced in 1930 included the 16/50 (2.1 litres), the Snipe (3½-litres) and a long-wheelbase Pullman version. The larger, luxury saloons then dominated the Humber range throughout the 1930s.

Humber's financial problems were solved when the Rootes Group took control of the concern in 1932. In 1933 a smaller Humber 12 was introduced, while in 1936 the largest six-cylinder model had an engine capacity of over four litres.

As World War II approached, the stately six-cylinder Humbers featured hydraulic brakes and independent front suspension, although sidevalve engines were fitted. The 4.1-litre Super Snipe was introduced at this time, and Humber

Snipes were used as staff cars by the Allies throughout the war.

When hostilities ceased, the pre-war models were reintroduced, together with a new, four-cylinder, 1.9-litre sidevalve Hawk, which owed a great deal to the 1939 Hillman Fourteen saloon.

Overhead-valve engines were used throughout the Humber range of Hawk (four-cylinder, 70bhp, 2267cc), Super Snipe and Pullman (six-cylinder, 113/116bhp, 4139cc), from 1952/3.

A rebodied, unitary construction Hawk was introduced in 1957, and a similarly styled Super Snipe (originally 2650cc, later 2965cc), in 1959. Saloon, limousine and estate-car versions of both models were produced.

The Humber Sceptre was announced in January 1963, being little more than a badge-engineered luxury version of the Hillman Super Minx/Singer Vogue, and fitted with an 85bhp 1592cc engine. The

88bhp 1725cc Sceptre was, from late 1967, the top model in the Rootes Group's Arrow range, in saloon and estate-car form.

The Humber name finally disappeared in the autumn of 1976, after the Chrysler takeover of Rootes.

Above: 1950s Hawk at the start of the overland journey to New Zealand

Below: 1964 Humber Super Snipe
Bottom: 1965 1725cc Humber Sceptre

Hyundai

Korea
1968 to date

Hyundai – Korea's largest industrial concern with interests in shipping and civil engineering – started assembling British Ford cars and trucks under licence in 1968.

By 1973 the company was building more than a third of Korea's vehicles and the next move was to graduate from assembly to production.

Most of the financial backing came from Barclays Bank in Britain and other London financial organizations.

George Turnbull, who had served his apprenticeship with the Standard Motor Co. and later became managing director of the Austin Morris division of the then British Leyland Motor Corporation, was chosen to mastermind the development and design of Hyundai's first car.

It was styled by Giugiaro and engineered by Ital Design in Turin. Bodies were partly built in France and most of the dies came from British Leyland.

The car used a 1238cc Mitsubishi engine and running gear and was announced as the Hyundai Pony in London in November 1974.

Production began late in 1975 and a target figure of 56,000 was met by the end of 1976. The figure reached 103,000 and a

decade later it was close to 400,000.

A slightly revised version of the Pony was launched in 1982, still with Mitsubishi running gear, but with an optional 92bhp 1439cc engine.

The range was extended in 1983 with the introduction of the Stellar saloon with

Top: 1981 Hyundai Pony 1400 GLS

Above: The Hyundai Pony of the early 1980s was a neat hatchback with a traditional rear-wheel-drive mechanical layout. The cars offered good value for money, and found many enthusiastic owners. This is a five-door, 1982 example.

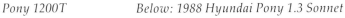

Above: 1982 Hyundai Pony 1200T   *Below: 1988 Hyundai Pony 1.3 Sonnet*

either the 1439cc engine or 1597cc unit.

Hyundai made significant inroads into export markets in the mid-1980s, selling cars to Canada and becoming the fastest-growing export marque in the U.S.

The new Pony sub-compact introduced to the U.K. in 1985 (called Excel in the U.S.) was totally different from its predecessor, having front-wheel-drive with a transverse engine, and was offered in both saloon and hatchback forms.

Four years later, with export sales of its small car falling, Hyundai entered the compact market segment with its Sonata saloon. This was initially powered by a Mitsubishi-designed 2.4-litre 110bhp four-cylinder engine, but later there was the option of a single-overhead-cam V6.

Right: 1989 model Hyundai Stellar saloon
Below: 1984 Hyundai Stellar 1600 GSL

Like the other Korean motor manufacturers, Hyundai's foreign market image and sales improved dramatically during the nineties. In the mid-1990s, Hyundai was Korea's biggest car manufacturer, producing over a million cars per year. The old range dragged on a little past its sell-by date but was gradually replaced with all-new models.

The ancient Pony, which had previously been the company's mainstay, finally received some curves in 1994, but retained the old model's 12-valve Mitsubishi motors. The other models followed suit.

New to the range, though, was the S Coupé. It had sporting pretensions and was even available with a powerful turbo motor. Unfortunately, the chassis couldn't quite keep up and the car was not a great success. It was revamped for 1996 with new ultra-modern and curvaceous styling and vastly improved handling. The new car used Hyundai's own new 16-valve engines with

Above: 1997 Hyundai Accent 1.5 MVi

Left: Hyundai Accent 1.5 GLSi

Right: The Lantra saloon

Below: 1997 Hyundai Coupé

Above: Hyundai Sonata 2.0 CD
Left: Hyundai Lantra estate

power outputs ranging from 114 to 139bhp. It was completely transformed and universally praised by the press and soon showed itself to be popular with buyers too. The four-door Lantra shared the same floorpan as the Coupé and gained the new engines at the same time.

Above: Hyundai Sonata V6

Imperial

U.S.A.
1954–1975

Although Imperial only became a make in its own right in 1954, the name had been used for luxury Chryslers since 1926. The reason for the separation was to create a more prestigious image for Imperials, along the lines of Cadillac's De Ville series and Ford's Lincoln range.

Above: 1930 Chrysler CG Imperial 8
Right: 1972 Chrysler Imperial Le Baron
Below right: 1974 Imperial Le Baron

Basically the cars were still just big Chryslers and used the overhead-valve V8, announced in 1951. The company's products were, in the late 1940s and early 1950s, noted for being very well put together and having excellent interiors, but to be rather plainly styled. Flite Sweep

Below: Luxury Chryslers from 1926 were designated 'Imperial'. During the 1920s and 1930s, elegant Le Baron coachwork featured on the cars, and the name was revived in the 1950s for prestigious Imperial models. This is a Chrysler Imperial of 1932.

bodywork, introduced in 1955, gave the cars a more modern appearance and increased their popularity, and also in that year disc brakes were fitted as standard.

During the 1920s and 1930s the famous LeBaron firm of coachbuilders had been responsible for Imperial bodies and that name was revived in 1957 to add prestige to the more expensive models. By 1960 some models were offered with luxuries such as automatically swivelling seats and power-operated vent windows.

Unitary-construction methods came in

by 1967 and four years later anti-lock brakes were standardized, the first such system in America. Engine power had risen to 335bhp, but this dropped to 225bhp in the early 1970s.

In 1974 Chrysler made a loss of over U.S. $52 million and the following year the decision was made to discontinue the Imperial name, which was achieving only one-fifth of Lincoln's sales. The LeBaron name, however, was revived in the early 1980s using Chrysler and Mitsubishi engines and front-wheel-drive.

Invicta

Great Britain 1925–1938; 1946–1950

Noel Campbell Macklin (father of the racing driver Lance Macklin) had already built the Eric Campbell and the Silver Hawk cars before his first Invicta appeared in 1925. Macklin had been impressed by the tremendous torque of an American Doble steam car and made his own car sufficiently flexible to run most of the time in top gear.

The original 1925 Invicta, with its handsome square-cut radiator and rivets down the bonnet-hinge line, was powered by a 2.6-litre six-cylinder Meadows engine, but in 1926 the engine capacity was increased to three litres and two years later to 4½ litres in an attempt further to increase low-speed torque. The company was financed by Oliver Lyle (of Tate and Lyle) and Earl Fitzwilliam, formerly of Sheffield Simplex, with design work by William Watson.

Above: 1927 Invicta 3-litre
Below: The 'Doctor's Coupé' version of the same car

Below: The famous 4500S of 1931 was extremely capable, and in the hands of professional drivers like Donald Healey its underslung chassis for good weight distribution and torquey engine made it more than a match for Continental rally competition.

THE 4½ LITRE MULLINER SALOON

Left: 1933 4½-litre Mulliner
Above: 1933 1½-litre

In 1930 two versions of the car became available, the high-chassis model and the graceful 100mph (160km/h) underslung-chassis model. Invicta cars were kept in the public eye by Violet and Evelyn Cordery with their long-distance timed runs, and by Donald Healey who did extremely well in international events with a win in the 1931 Monte Carlo Rally and a second place the following year, driving a 4½-litre S Type.

However, the Depression was beginning to bite by this time, with production of the 4½-litre cars almost ceasing by 1935; and even the new 1½-litre six-cylinder Blackburne-powered 12/45 car launched some three years earlier was not doing well. It was overweight and underpowered and although this was to some extent remedied in the 1932 Supercharged 12/90, in 1933 Macklin sold out to Lord Fitzwilliam and helped to form the new Railton Motor Company. Three new Invictas were announced for 1936 but they were little more than rebodied French Darracqs and the project came to nothing.

The Invicta name was revived in 1946 with the introduction of the Black Prince, with its twin-overhead-camshaft three-litre Meadows engine, an untried Brockhouse automatic transmission and independent torsion-bar suspension all round, but the cars were very expensive and only a handful were sold. In 1950 the goodwill and the remaining cars and parts were bought by A.F.N. Ltd., makers of the Frazer-Nash.

Isotta-Fraschini

Italy
1900–1949

Isotta-Fraschini, not to be confused with bubble-car barons Isetta, were often thought of during their between-the-wars heyday as the ultimate practitioners of Italian automotive art.

Ironically, however, it was only their very strong and often-changing links with other countries that gave them their pre-eminence and their profits – the former surviving rather longer and more reliably than the latter.

The firm was founded in 1898 by car enthusiast Vincenzo Fraschini and moneyed lawyer Cesare Isotta, at first to import French Renault and De Dion cars into Italy. Two years later they officially named their partnership Societa Milanese d'Automobili Isotta, Fraschini & Cia and started building their first home-grown product – but from imported parts and certainly from borrowed ideas.

However, they soon started developing an identity of their own and after engineer Giustino Cattaneo, the man behind many of their best products, joined in 1905, sales boomed and models proliferated. In 1907,

however, a cash shortfall found them again looking abroad, this time to Lorraine-Dietrich who became the firm's partners until 1909.

During these years the marque was starting to build a reputation in racing, with a few notable successes, particularly in the U.S.A. These provided the foundation for sales success in America, which was capitalized on only after World

Above: A 1910 50/65hp

Above: The 1906 18/22 was competent but hardly unique
Below: The Type 8, introduced in 1919

War I which the company spent building all manner of engines for everything from armoured trucks to boats.

But soon afterwards, and by an inspired piece of marketing, they hauled themselves firmly up-market to take on the limousine makers such as Rolls-Royce and Mercedes (which the distinctive radiator grille most resembled).

American film stars, celebrities and tycoons hurried to buy the prestigious Isotta-Fraschini Type 8 which was first introduced in 1919 – with only the mechanicals being supplied by the company themselves, the variation in body styles was extensive. Italian and French styling houses vied with American and British coachbuilders to make more and more extreme and ostentatious bodies for the powerful 5.9-litre engine and quite advanced chassis which the skilled engineer Cattaneo had designed.

The names behind the company fell by the wayside in the early 1920s, with Vincenzo Fraschini leaving in 1922, a year

after his brother Oreste, also involved with the firm, died. At the same time Isotta sold his holding. The new owner, Mille Miglia founder and enthusiast Count Lodovico Mazzotti, continued with the luxury-car market but diversified into aero-engines as well, again scoring notable success in the U.S.A.

This rebounded rather negatively on the car side of the business; as the aircraft industry flourished it took more of the

Above: By 1929, the year of this model, the founders had left the company
Below right: The post-war Type 8C

firm's resources and the Type 8 was left to stagnate expensively until very nearly killed off by the Depression.

Ford expressed an interest in the firm, but some manoeuvring by Fiat stopped that partnership ever bearing fruit, and in 1933 the company effectively went

bankrupt, to be rescued by aircraft manufacturer Caproni who valued Isotta-Fraschini's aeronautical expertise.

During World War II this was put to good use by Mussolini's forces who flew Isotta-engined aircraft, drove Isotta-engineered trucks and patrolled in Isotta-powered boats. It was a tribute to the versatility of the company's designs, but a bad move in terms of post-war credibility.

They were only to return to car manufacture briefly, with the 8C Monterosa in the late 1940s. Ambitious and advanced, it nonetheless sold only six models before the firm yet again went into liquidation. The trucks and buses they had been manufacturing hadn't been enough to keep the wolf from the door, so they folded up. The company now makes engines and industrial drivetrains for all sorts of applications.

The expensive and immense Type 8 of the 1920s was the finest flowering of the company's push into the luxury car market. It was bodied by all the great coachbuilders. The price may have been high, but the steering was heavy and the brakes dubious at best.

Isuzu

Japan
1953 to date

Although the present Isuzu company dates from 1953, it can trace its ancestry back to 1916 when the Tokyo Ishikawajiama Ship Building and Engineering Company merged with the Tokyo Gas and Electric Company to produce motor vehicles. In 1918 the company signed an agreement with British manufacturer Wolseley for production and marketing rights of its cars in the Far East, and the first Japanese-built Wolseley appeared in 1922.

An independent company was set up in 1929 to build cars to original designs. This was initially called the Ishikawajiama Automotive Works Company, then the Automobile Industries Company, and it used the trade names Sumida and Chiyoda. These were later abandoned in favour of Isuzu, after the Japanese river.

Above: The 1943 PA10

In 1937 Automobile Industries became known as the Tokyo Automobile Industries Company, and in 1949 it changed identity yet again to become Isuzu Motor Ltd.

In 1953 the company reached an agreement with the British Rootes organization to build Hillman cars under licence. The first cars were assembled later the same year, and by 1957 the Minx was fully sourced and built in Japan.

Isuzu's first original design was the Bellel, launched in 1961. This was a traditional four-door saloon with obvious Western influences in its styling, and was available with either a 1471cc petrol engine or a two-litre diesel (making it the first-ever diesel-powered Japanese car).

Above: The 1963 Bellet four-door saloon   *Below: The successful coupé version*

Two years later came the slightly smaller Bellet (also available as a two-door coupé), then in 1966 appeared the attractive 117 coupé. The 1584cc Florian saloon was launched in 1967 with body design by Ghia, and a double-overhead camshaft engine with twin carburettors.

The later 1960s saw a marked downturn in Isuzu's fortunes, however. Production dropped from 39,776 cars in 1968 to 18,815 in 1970, and the company began to seek collaboration with other manufacturers in an effort to reduce its costs. Fuji, Mitsubishi and Nissan were all involved for a time, but it was not until 1971 that General Motors took a 34 per cent share in Isuzu to herald a dramatic revival of the latter's fortunes. The first car to appear as a result of this union was the 1974 Gemini, an Isuzu-built version of the contemporary Opel Kadett-Chevrolet Chevette. The car

The Isuzu Piazza, which was launched in 1981, is the most powerful Isuzu car to date with its 180bhp 1994cc four-cylinder engine and its optional turbocharger. However, it has enjoyed only moderate success despite styling by Giugiaro and favourable press coverage.

Above: The Isuzu/Aska

was powered by a 1584 or 1817cc engine and transmission was by four- or five-speed manual gearbox or a three-speed automatic.

The Gemini was revised in 1979, then in 1984 it was totally redesigned to offer front-wheel-drive in a package based on

Below: The Gemini, for export to the U.S.A.

Above: The ever-increasing off-road market is catered for too

General Motors' R-Car design. The very first front-wheel-drive Isuzu, however, was the 1983 Florian/Aska.

The only Isuzu car to be marketed in Britain (as opposed to the four-wheel-drive Trooper, and the Bedford-badged KB pickup and Midi panel van) was the Piazza (badged in the U.S.A. as the Impulse). Designed by Giorgio Giugiaro and launched in 1981, it was as dramatically styled for its time as had been the 117 coupé in 1966.

Itala

Italy
1904–1934

The Ceirano brothers had a hand in the development of over seven different makes of car, including the beginnings of Fiat. In 1903 Matteo Ceirano, looking for competition glory, left his elder brother's firm to set up his own marque with Guido Bigio, Grosso Campana, Giovanni Carenzi, Leone Fubini and Angelo Moriondo in premises in Turin.

By 1904 the company gained victory with what was essentially its first machine, driven by Ceirano in the Susa-Mont Cenisio hill-climb. The following year Giovanni Battista Raggio won the Coppa Florio in a 15.3-litre car and in 1906 an Itala took the Targa Florio with Allesandro Cagno at the wheel.

The workforce expanded as sales took off. Queen Mother Margherita of Italy owned no less than five of the cars and in 1907, Prince Scipione Borghese won the Peking-to-Paris marathon by a three-week margin. Fame also led to imitations – in particular from the British Weigel and B.S.A. companies.

Until World War I Itala offered a wide, complex range of vehicles, and was experimenting with rotary-valve engines. Bigio was killed testing one intended for the 1913 French Grand Prix. Ceirano had left the company in 1905 to start S.P.A. the following year.

Disastrous war-time contracts for Hispano-Suiza aero-engines left Itala in a perilous financial state. The 51S model won the 1922 and 1923 Targa Florio, but by 1925 Itala was being run by receivers appointed by the Italian government. Even the Tipo 61, designed by ex-Fiat man

The racing pedigree of this marque was never in doubt, even from its earliest days. Probably its finest hour was in 1907 when a 35/45 model of this type, piloted by Prince Scipione Borghese, co-driver Luigi Barzini and mechanic Ettore Guizzardi, won the Peking to Paris race by a huge margin, boosting sales immensely.

Above: Grandeur and grace – the 1907 model

Cappa, could not revive the company and a new V12 racer failed to get off the ground.

Two attempts at updating the 61 both failed, as did various reorganizations of the company in 1929 and 1931. It finally closed down at the end of 1934.

Above: 1908 12-litre racing model

Below: A pair of 12hp Italas sold in 1912

Below: 1910 75hp six-cylinder Itala

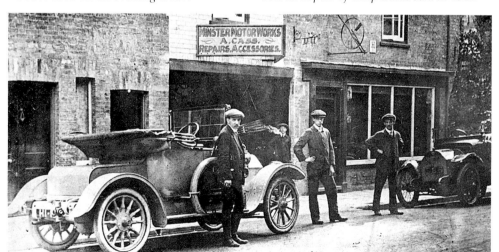

Jaguar

Great Britain 1954 to date

Jaguar's origins can be traced back to the early 1920s when William Lyons – who was later to become Sir William – set up the Swallow Sidecar Company.

He initially planned to become an apprentice at the Vickers shipyards but his father persuaded him to train with Crossley Motors in Manchester, augmenting his training with an evening engineering course at Manchester Technical College.

He again changed direction and returned to his native Blackpool to help his father's piano restoration business. Lyon's had been a keen motorcyclist for some years and later he took a job as a salesman for a Sunbeam dealer.

A chance meeting led to a further change. In 1921, William Walmsley moved into a house near Lyons' home, building aluminium sports sidecars from the garage. Lyons bought a sidecar and suggested that, as a team, they could build up the business.

Walmsley agreed reluctantly and they began working from premises on the top floor of an electrical equipment factory in Blackpool. Their company – the Swallow Sidecar Co. – was officially registered in September 1922.

Business boomed and, four years later, they formed the Swallow Sidecar and Coachbuilding Co. and moved to larger premises.

Lyons chose his own Austin Seven as a guinea pig and the company developed a special body for it. The car emerged in 1927 as the Austin Swallow – a two-seater with optional hinged hard top – and it quickly went into production.

It was followed soon afterwards by the Morris-based Cowley Swallow, and the company also built bodies based on Alvis and Clyno chassis.

The expansion continued and the company had 50 workers by 1928, building two cars a day and 100 sidecars a week.

More space was need and the business moved to a former ammunition works in Coventry where Lyons set a production target of 50 cars a week. Larger models were built, including several on Fiat chassis.

The company made its first appearance at the Motor Show in 1929 and two years later production was up to 30 cars a day.

October 1931 was a significant month for the company. It launched the SS1 – the first car to use a purpose-built chassis with a Swallow body. It used Standard 16hp running gear and was competitively priced at £310.

The smaller SS11 was launched at the same time, this model utilizing the 1052cc Standard Little Nine running gear. A total of 776 cars were sold in 1932.

Below: Standard Swallow of 1929
Bottom: 1936 Jaguar SS100

Above: Swallow sidecar of the 1920s

To simplify matters, the car section was separated from the sidecar operation in 1933 to become SS Cars Ltd.

The company had already produced drop-head versions of four-seaters but the first true sports car came in March 1935. It was the SS90, a two-seater with a 20hp 2663cc engine.

The Jaguar name appeared six months later with the introduction of the 2663cc overhead-valve SS100 Jaguar. The Jaguar suffix was then adopted for all SS models.

Walmsley and Lyons split up after many disagreements, Walmsley leaving to join the Airlite Trailer Co. and Lyons becoming major shareholder in SS Cars Ltd. when it was floated as a public company in January 1935.

The Swallow Coachbuilding Co. was put into voluntary liquidation and, with £10,000 nominal capital, Lyons set up the private company Swallow Coachbuilding Co. (1935) Ltd. to continue sidecar production.

By now, SS Cars was producing about 1,500 cars a year and had some 600 workers. The Sunbeam Motor Car Co. had gone bankrupt and Lyons tried to buy it but Rootes beat him to the deal.

SS1 and SS11 models were dropped in 1936. But over the following two years, plans to introduce new models were hampered by troublesome all-metal bodywork. However, SS Cars managed to

Above: 1982 XJ and 1937 SS Jaguars

Left: 1939 1.8 SS Saloon

make a small profit and production had exceeded 5,000 cars before the beginning of World War II.

The war years kept the factory busy making centre sections for Meteor aircraft, repairing and servicing bombers, building about 10,000 sidecars and experimenting with lightweight vehicles which could be dropped by parachute. Most of Coventry suffered tremendous damage from bombing but SS Cars escaped relatively undamaged.

A major reorganization after the war led to Jaguar Cars Ltd. being set up in March 1945. Swallow was sold to the Helliwell group (later the name was bought by Tube Investments and then Watsonian – a famous name which is still registered).

Jaguar resumed production in July 1945 but in February 1947 fire caused £100,000 worth of damage to its factory.

Jaguar's models had so far been essentially pre-war designs with 1.8-litre four-cylinder engines and 2.7-litre or 3.5-litre sixes. The sixes were Jaguar's own and the old Standard four was dropped in 1949.

1939 version of SS100. Introduced in 1935, the SS100 was the first model to bear the Jaguar name. The 2663cc overhead valve six-cylinder engine made the car capable of a genuine 160km/h (100mph). Jaguar and speed were now synonymous.

Lyons entrusted the engineering work to former Humber employee William Heynes who had joined SS Cars as chief engineer in 1934. Together with Harry Weslake, he first re-designed the Standard engines and later created the classic Jaguar sixes and V12 with engineers such as Claude Baily and Walter Hassan.

Jaguar created a sensation when the XK120 was launched in October 1948. It was a true 120mph (193km/h) sports car with 160bhp from a 3.4-litre double-overhead-cam engine, and all for a commendably low £1273. A total of 12,055 were sold with very few going to British customers. In fact, 92 per cent were exported and in 1952 the figure was 96 per cent, over 60 per cent of those cars going to the United States. Its replacement in October 1954 was a worthy successor – the 190bhp XK140.

Post-war sensation, the 1949 XK120 Jaguar. Its 3.4-litre double overhead cam straight six engine gave it a 193km/h (120mph) top speed – breathtaking for its time. The modern straight six Jaguar engine is a direct descendant.

Above: 1952 Long Nose C-Type

Jaguar had realized the value of the publicity which could be gained from track successes. Factory XKs were racing in the early 1950s followed by purpose-built C- and D-Type racing cars. The C-Type clocked up one Le Mans 24-Hour win in 1951 with four more victories going to D-Types in 1953, 1955, 1956 and 1957. Jaguar then withdrew from major participation in racing, partly because of its involvement in the 1955 Le Mans disaster.

The image built by the XK models and racers gave a tremendous boost to saloon-car sales. The Mark VII, launched in 1951 with the twin-cam engine as a replacement for earlier pushrod units, proved extremely popular and over 30,000 were built up to 1957. It was replaced by the improved Mark VIII and then the Mark IX with a 3.8-litre engine and power-assisted steering as standard.

Above: 1950 3½-litre Mk V dhc
Below: The Mk VII launched 1951

Profits had been healthy enough to allow the company to move into the Brown's Lane factory which had formerly been occupied by Daimler, providing over a million square feet of production area. The move took place between 1950 and 1952.

The 1950s were flourishing years for Jaguar with 1956 being particularly memorable – William Lyons was knighted.

The company had announced the unitary-construction 2.4-litre saloon at the end of 1955, later dubbing it the Mark I, and it was joined by a 3.8-engined version in 1959. The same engine was also used in the mighty XK150 which was introduced in May 1957.

Below: 1954 XK140 fhc

Below: 1956 XK140 Roadster
Below centre: 1957 XK SS

Above: 1954 XK120 Coupé

Above: 1960 XK150 dhc
Below: 1960 XK150 fhc
Bottom: 1959-61 3781cc Mk IX

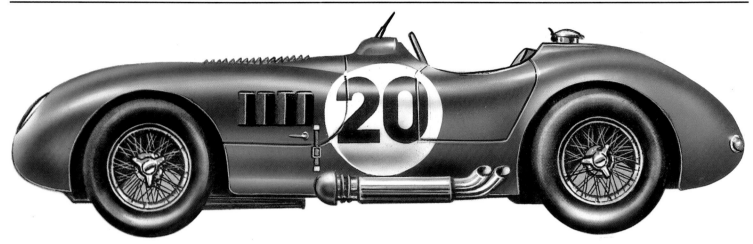

The company suffered another disastrous fire in February 1957 and almost a quarter of the factory was destroyed with damage put at £3.5 million. But to Jaguar's credit, production was back to normal within two months and in June 1960 it bought the Daimler Co. for £3.4 million from the B.S.A. group. Daimler production continued but the cars eventually became badge-engineered Jaguars.

The Mark II saloon was introduced in October 1959, eventually being available in 2.4-, 3.4- and 3.8-litre guises, and finally ending up as the 240.

One of the company's most famous cars – the E-Type – was launched in March 1961 to replace the XK150. It was mechanically similar but heavily based on the racing D-Type. It was a genuine 150mph (240km/h) sports car for less than £2,100.

Above: 1951 Jaguar C-Type racing car based on the XK120. It won the 1951 Le Mans 24-Hour race, gaining tremendous prestige for the marque. Jaguar went on to win Le Mans in 1953-55-56-57 with the subsequent D-Type version.

The saloon-car range was expanded with the cavernous Mark X in 1962 which featured independent rear suspension and unitary body construction.

Jaguar wanted to bridge the gap between the relatively compact Mark II and the larger Mark X and the company introduced the S-Type in 1964. It was basically a long-booted Mark II with the Mark X's independent rear suspension and it came with either a 3.4- or 3.8-litre engine.

Above right: 1960 Mk II Jaguar saloon
Right: 1963 S-Type saloon
Below: 1961 Series I E-Type

The famous double-overhead-cam straight-six was stretched to 4.2 litres in 1965 and was used in the Mark X and then the 420 saloon of 1967, an improved version of the S-Type. The 4.2 also replaced the 3.8-litre engine in the E-Type in 1965.

Jaguar merged with the British Motor Corporation in July 1966 to form British Motor Holdings with Sir William Lyons retaining control of Jaguar. B.M.H. merged with Leyland in May 1968 and Jaguar became part of the new British Leyland Motor Corporation.

Above: 1966 4.2-litre Mk X saloon

Below: 1968 Series II E-Type Coupé

Above: 1967 340 saloon

Below: 1966 420 saloon

Below: 1966 V12 XJ13

Below: 1967 S-Type saloon

The hugely successful XJ6 saloon was Jaguar's first product as part of British Leyland. It was introduced in September 1968 with either a 2.8- or 4.2-litre engine (the smaller unit later earning a reputation for being troublesome and subsequently being dropped) and helped the company set a new production record of 32,000 cars in 1970.

Jaguar had experimented with a rear-engined racer in the mid-1960s, using a four-cam V12 engine. The racer was stillborn but the work was not wasted because the E-Type was offered in 5.3-litre V12 form in 1971.

The XJ6 also came in for the V12 treatment and the XJ12 was introduced in 1972. It was in such demand that, for a while, secondhand models were selling for more than the new price.

A total of over 72,500 E-Types in various forms had been built when the famous model was replaced by the stylish XJ-S 5.3-litre four-seater luxury sports saloon in 1975.

Sir William Lyons retired as managing director and was succeeded by 'Lofty' England who had run Jaguar's competition department in the 1950s.

Geoffrey Robinson succeeded him in 1974 but Jaguar's independence was questioned by the government-sponsored Ryder Report in 1975 which examined Leyland's problems. Robinson resigned.

Above: 1968-69 240 saloon   *Below: 1969 Series I XJ6*

Below: Series III E-Type. Introduced in 1961, the 3.8-litre E-Type was the glamour car of the 1960s. Capable of over 240km/h (150mph), this triple carburettor wonder was finally produced in V12 form. E-Types were direct descendants of the racing D-Type.

Above: 1971 Series III V12 E-Type
Right: 1975 Series II XJ6
Below: 1973 Series I XJ12

Right: 1975 5.3-litre XJ Coupé
Below: 1975 V12 XJS

Below: 1968 2.8-litre XJ6. Introduced in September that year and also available in 4.2-litre form, it was voted Car of the Year.

Leyland enjoyed a tremendous revival under Sir Michael Edwardes and Jaguar regained its identity to such a degree that it was known simply as Jaguar Cars from 1978.

John Egan, formerly of Massey-Ferguson, became chairman of Jaguar in April 1980 with the company becoming Jaguar Cars Ltd. Sir William Lyons remained as honorary president until his death at the age of 83 in 1985, the year after Jaguar was returned from state-ownership to the private sector.

Egan treated Jaguar's individuality as a priority and his enthusiasm extended to the racing involvement with the XJ-R Sports Prototype racing cars built by Tom Walkinshaw Racing. One of these won the Le Mans 24-Hours race in 1988.

Under Egan's leadership, Jaguar greatly improved quality control which had previously lapsed and damaged the company's reputation. Sales improved in the all-important American market.

Below: 1980 Series III XJ12

Left: 1980 XJ saloon

An XJ6 replacement – the Jaguar Sovereign – was launched in October 1986 with new 2.9- and 3.6-litre engines, the latter enlarged in 1989 to 4.0-litres. And the XJ-S continued to sell well with the V12 convertible heading the range from March 1988.

But the overall success of Jaguar sales during the 1980s grew dangerously

dependent on the U.S. market, and by 1988 alterations in the dollar/pound exchange rate had seriously reduced profits. Accepting that his company lacked the resources to independently develop crucial new models, Sir John Egan entered into discussions with G.M. This prompted a 'hostile' take-over bid by Ford, and in November 1989 Jaguar Cars became a wholly-owned subsidiary of Ford of Great Britain.

Left: 1983 5.3-litre XJS HE
Below: V12 long-distance racers

Below: 1985 XJSC HE V12

Below: 1986 XJS Cabriolet

Below: 1986 3.6 Sovereign 'XJ40'

Above: 1989 2.9-litre Jaguar XJ6　　　*Below: 1989 5343cc V12 XJS Coupé*　　　*Right: Jaguar at Le Mans '89*

Below: Jaguar XJS, introduced 1975 and still in production. A luxury 2+2 two-door coupé, it featured a 5343cc ohc V12 fuel injection engine, disc brakes all round and air conditioning. A High Efficiency (HE) version was introduced in 1981.

Top left: 1988 Jaguar Sovereign

Top right: V12 XJR-S special

Above: 1997 XK8 Coupé

Following the takeover, Ford knew it would have a lot to do to get Jaguar back into profit. In 1992 Jaguar had to cut production and its workforce. This was a major embarrassment to Ford, who saw losses of a million dollars a day from a company for which it had paid $2.5 billion. The parent company bravely carried the burden and continued to contribute money and expertise to a new model programme which would see new engines and a new coupé, as well as a new small saloon by the end of the century.

A new XJ6 came in 1994 and immediately boosted Jaguar's flagging worldwide sales figures. The new car used Jaguar's AJ16 engine in an all-new, retro-styled body. Top of the range was the 4.0-litre XJR with a supercharger and 320bhp. There was also a V12 version, as well as Daimler-badged derivatives.

The replacement for the XJ-S didn't arrive until 1996. The new car was called the XK8 and used an all-new 4.0-litre V8 engine. It owed its sleek looks to its famous predecessor, the E-type, and was launched at Geneva as the E-type had been 35 years earlier. It was greatly praised by the press and sold

Below: The 4.0-litre XJ-S convertible

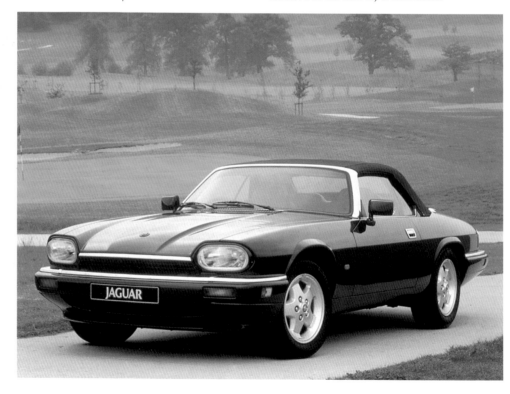

much better than the aged XJ-S had done. Both coupé and convertible body styles were available. The new V8 engine was fitted to the rest of the Jaguar range.

As the turn of the century draws nearer, so too does the much awaited launch of the new small Jaguar, codenamed X200. After speculation that the new car would be built outside Britain, it was revealed that a new factory would be set up in Birmingham to build the new car. It was reported in the motoring press that the new car would have retro styling, with a grille shaped like that on the old MkII.

As part of Ford 2000, Ford's plan to reduce the number of different platforms used by all of its car manufacturing divisions, it is possible that new Fords may share their underpinnings and possibly engines with the new Jaguars.

Top left: 1997 Jaguar Sovereign

Top right: 1997 Jaguar XJ12

Left: 4.0-litre XJ Sport

Below: 1990 XJ220

Jensen

Great Britain 1935–1976

Car enthusiasts Allan and Richard Jensen were relative youngsters when their father gave them a 1923 Austin Chummy.

Yet they rebuilt it as a sporting two-seater and took it to a hillclimb at Shelsley Walsh where Standard Motor Co. chief engineer Arthur Wilde was impressed enough to ask them to build him a similar body on a Standard Nine chassis.

The car was completed in 1928 which led to Allan being asked to design a production version for Avon Bodies, called the Avon Standard.

He and his brother later joined W. J. Smith and Sons, a small bodybuilding company, and scored such a success manufacturing bodies that they took over the company as Jensen Motors Ltd. in 1934.

The first car to carry the Jensen name was a 3.6-litre Ford V8-engined four-seater tourer, launched in 1935. Customers included Clark Gable.

Top: 1937 V8 3.6-litre
Left: 1939 four-door S-Type
Above: 1950 Nash-powered PW

1938 Jensen convertible with 120bhp 3.6-litre Ford V8 engine and two speed Columbia rear axle. Film star Clark Gable indulged himself with one of these glamorous sports tourers. Jensen continued to use American engines.

The four-door S-Type was added in 1935 and continued in production until 1939. The Type H, a long-wheelbase version of the S, was also made.

World War II saw Jensen building ambulances, fire engines and amphibian tank conversions, and car production resumed after the war.

The first post-war car was the large PW saloon with a Nash engine. Jensen also formed links with Austin and eventually built bodies for the 1950 Austin A40.

Expansion dictated a move to a new factory in West Bromwich in 1956 and contracts included bodies for the big Austin-Healey and Volvo P1800 sports car.

One of the most memorable Jensens was the Chrysler-powered CV8 of 1963 which offered luxury and high performance. It was offered with Ferguson four-wheel-drive two years later and anti-lock brakes by 1966.

With the Jensen brothers approaching retirement, chief engineer Kevin Beattie orchestrated the next-generation Jensen – the Touring-designed Interceptor of 1966 – also available with four-wheel-drive in FF form.

But Jensen was in serious financial trouble for several reasons. The Rootes takeover by Chrysler saw the end of Sunbeam Alpine production which robbed Jensen of the contract to build bodies for the V8-derivative, the Tiger. Jensen was also hit by the phasing out of the Austin-Healey.

After a takeover by merchant bank William Brandt in June 1968, Donald Healey and his son Geoffrey were appointed to the board which led to the Jensen-Healey being introduced in 1972. It used the Lotus-developed 16-valve slant-four, a problematical and unreliable unit.

The car never sold well. The oil crisis had also badly hit Interceptor sales.

Jensen went into receivership in September 1975, the victim of the oil crisis, labour problems and increasing U.S. legislation. The company finally closed in May 1976.

However, the name has been kept alive with Jensen Cars, set up to produce Interceptors to customers' orders with production under way by 1986 – at a mere one a month.

Top: 1956 Jensen 541 4-litre   *Above: 1963 CV8 5.9-litre*

Below: 1972 Interceptor III

Left: 1974 Interceptor III convertible

Below left: 1975 Jensen-Healey GT 2.0

Top: 1973 193km/h (120mph) Jensen-Healey
Above: 1976 Lotus-powered GT
Below: 1988 Series IV Interceptor

Jowett

Great Britain
1906–1953

The Bradford, Yorkshire, firm of Jowett was started by two brothers – William and Benjamin Jowett – who made vee-twin engines for other firms before building their own vehicles. Their first car was built in 1906, and their famous flat-twin engine was to be built continuously from 1910 to 1953.

Their first designs evolved into a production two-cylinder, two-seater car in 1913. The 816cc sidevalve engine (increased in size to 907cc after World War I) drove via a three-speed gearbox.

The hard-working twin-cylinder engine performed well, and proved to be extremely reliable. It was also capable of returning excellent fuel consumption figures.

Above: 1911 Jowett 8hp two-seater

An electric starter was fitted from 1923, and a four-seater (Long Four) model was introduced, followed by a saloon version in 1926. Four-wheel brakes and a detachable cylinder head formed part of the specification in 1929, in which year the firm also introduced the fabric-bodied Black Prince model.

The Jowetts of the early 1930s, including the sporting Kestrel model of 1934 and the twin-carburettor Weasel, still had twin-cylinder engines, although four-speed transmission was fitted, together with a centrifugal clutch and freewheel assembly, from 1935.

Four cylinders first appeared in a production Jowett – the Ten saloon, with a flat-four engine of 1166cc, in 1936. However, the twins continued in production, with a slightly increased capacity from 1937 – 946cc instead of the 907cc used previously. As a comparison, the 8hp, 946cc twin-cylinder units produced 17bhp at 3,250rpm, while the 10hp four-cylinder gave 31bhp at 4,000rpm.

With the intervention of World War II, both the Eight and Ten were to disappear. However, the twin-cylinder engine, in 25bhp, 1000cc form, continued in production and was fitted to the Bradford van, which became renowned for its reliability.

A new model, the very advanced Javelin saloon, was introduced in 1947. Designed by Gerald Palmer, the streamlined and roomy Javelin featured a 1486cc flat-four engine developing 50bhp (later 53bhp). Citroën-inspired torsion-bar suspension gave excellent ride and handling qualities, and performance was brisk – sufficient to give a top speed of over 80mph (128km/h).

By the early 1950s Javelins were built at the rate of around 125 per week, together with some 135 Bradford vans.

A sophisticated sports version of the Javelin – the two-seater Jupiter – was introduced in 1950, and was capable of over 90mph (145km/h). The 100mph (160km/h) glassfibre bodied R4 Jupiter was a further development.

The Javelin-based cars competed successfully in many motor sport events,

Above: 1923 Jowett 7hp 'Short Two'
Below: A Jowett Jupiter of 1953

including the Monte Carlo Rally and Le Mans 24-Hour events.

Post-war Jowett bodies were built by Briggs Motor Bodies, in Doncaster, Yorkshire. Sadly, in 1953, Briggs was obliged to stop producing the bodies following declining Jowett sales, and the famous Bradford firm finally ceased production.

Kaiser

U.S.A.
1946–1955

The Kaiser company is generally considered to be the most successful post-war attempt by an independent manufacturer to break the Detroit-based domination of the American motor industry.

The Kaiser-Frazer Corporation was launched by Henry J. Kaiser, former World War II shipbuilder, and Joseph W. Frazer, who had been involved with both Willys-Overland and Graham-Paige.

Frazer initially rented the Willow Run premises, previously used for the war-time manufacture of B24 Liberator bombers by Henry Ford. The first prototype, shown to the public in 1946, displayed features which would later be adopted by the entire industry. Unfortunately, costs prevented Kaiser-Frazer from developing them for its first production model, the Custom Sedan. Two separate lines were offered until 1951, with Kaiser standard and Frazer luxury models.

The company did well up to 1949 when the major manufacturers introduced brand-new designs with which it simply could not compete. Sales dropped and money was borrowed to keep Kaiser-Frazer afloat. This led to arguments between the founders and Frazer all but resigned.

Left: 1948 Kaiser Special four-door sedan
Above: 1951 Frazer Vagabond three-door

Below: 1954 Kaiser Special four-door   *Above: 1952 two-door Henry J. Kaiser*

The launch of an economy car, the Henry J., was mistimed into a market that wanted luxury. Attempts by Sears Roebuck to boost sales with its own Allstate version had failed by 1953. The dramatically styled sedan of 1951 was an inspired design, but Kaiser-Frazer was rapidly getting left behind and was still not offering a V8 engine by 1952.

In 1954 Kaiser-Frazer merged with Willys-Overland, becoming Kaiser-Willys Sales Corporation and moving to Toledo, Ohio.

A new 161 glassfibre-bodied sports model did not succeed and in 1955 the firm closed, although the design was continued in Argentina for a further seven years.

Kissel

U.S.A.
1906–1930

William and George Kissel formed the Kissel Motor Co., having built an experimental vehicle in the family agricultural factory in 1905. The name was to undergo slight changes, from Kisselkar to Kissel Kar in 1908, then became plain Kissel after World War I.

They set up production in Hartford, Wisconsin, and were joined by engineer Herman Palmer and coachbuilder J. Friedrich Werner. Commercial vehicles with Waukesha or Wisconsin engines appeared in 1908. By this time the cars were mainly powered by Kissel engines, although a V12 Weidely was tried briefly in 1917, and later Lycoming straight-eights were offered. The general emphasis was on quality.

During World War I the company built four-wheel-drive military vehicles and carried out development work on the Liberty truck. Up to that time Kissel had no sporting aspirations, although its body styles were innovative. In 1918, however,

Below: 1924 6-55 Berline   *Top: 1920 6-45 Tourster*   *Above: 1920 6-45 Speedster*

Left: 1914-20 'All-Year' KisselKar

New York dealer Conover T. Silver designed the striking Silver Special Speedster. Two years later came the Gold Bug and during the early 1920s Kissels were noted as one of the most attractive American designs, although limited in production.

Sales began to decline towards the end of the 1920s, however, leading to unsuccessful contracts for taxis, then with Archie Andrews of New Era Motors to build Ruxtons in 1930. By the end of that year the latter deal had fallen through and Kissel's only option was receivership. The company was reorganized the following year as Kissel Industries and the Hartford works was used for the production of various engine parts until 1943, when it was sold to the West Bend Aluminum Co.

Below: 1927 Kissel 8-75 Speedster. Introduced in New York in 1919, it was nicknamed the Gold Bug because of its standard chrome/yellow finish, a name that stuck for subsequent speedsters. Power unit was a side valve 4.3-litre Six, later enlarged to 4.7 litres.

Lada

Russia
1970 to date

Lada is the name by which the Russian Zhiguli car is know on foreign markets. The company was founded with Fiat aid in 1970. The Togliattigrad works, west of Moscow, was fitted out with most of Fiat's 124 production facility and the new factory started production of a Fiat 124-based car with a rugged Soviet-designed engine. This first car, the type 2100, also known as the Riva, was produced well into the 1990s. High demand and little competition in its home country meant that very few changes were made during the long production run.

In 1979 Lada introduced a new four-wheel-drive model, the Niva, to Western markets. The rush of small Japanese off-roaders put the Niva in the shade as far as quality was concerned. But when the going got tough, this tough little Russian left them standing. It shared the engines of the Lada Riva saloon, but used an in-house 4wd system. Amazing axle articulation gave incredible traction in impossible conditions, but on-road handling lagged a long way

behind most competitors. The car's main attraction lay in its bargain-basement price.

A more modern offering was launched in 1984. The Samara had new engines, gearbox, body and front-wheel-drive but was cursed with a dreadful interior and poor finish. It lacked much in the way of dynamic qualities, with dull performance, indifferent handling and a bouncy ride. Many buyers stuck with the old Riva.

The company made another effort at a modern car in 1996. Called the 110, it was available with a choice of engines, including a couple of 16-valve units, one a 2.0-litre, 150bhp Opel unit.

Top: 1970 Lada 1200 saloon

Below: Lada Samara five-door hatchback

Above: Late-model Lada Niva 4x4

Below: 1996 Lada Riva estate and saloon

Lagonda

Great Britain
1906 to date

American Wilbur Gunn started by building motorcycles in a small workshop at the bottom of his garden in Staines, Middlesex.

He called the operation the Lagonda Engineering Company after Lagonda Creek near his home town of Springfield, Ohio.

He then started making tricars but production stopped in 1907. A receiver was called in to wind up the company.

Meanwhile, Gunn produced a few four-wheelers, including a 10hp vee-twin and 14/16hp Coventry-Simplex-engined car.

A new company, Lagonda Ltd., was formed in 1913 with finance from Henry Tollemache of the brewing family and with Gunn in charge. He introduced a small Lagonda of integral construction and with a 1099cc engine. About 200 were made up to 1916.

After World War I the 1099cc Lagonda was revived and a 1420cc engine was installed in 1921.

Lagonda completely changed direction in 1926 with the new 14/60. It featured a

Below: 1913 1100cc 11.1hp convertible   *Top: 1913 11.1hp Lagonda*   *Above: 1924 12/24 Lagonda*

twin-overhead-camshaft engine of nearly two litres and powerful Rubery brakes. It was expensive at £430 for a chassis, and Lagonda sales dropped from about 700 to 400 a year.

Subsequent models included the three-litre six of 1928 and a supercharged two-litre model in 1930. They helped lead to a racing programme with entries at Le Mans.

Lagonda's range became increasingly complex with cars such as the 1933 9hp Rapier, the 4½-litre M45, 1936 4½-litre Rapide, two-litre and three-litre models, and seasonal sales led to problems with

Above: 1929 six-cylinder 3-litre
Above right: 1924 12/24 saloon
Right: 1931 supercharged 2-litre

Lagonda Rapier of 1936. A 9hp Rapier was listed in 1933 and a twin cam 1100cc Rapier in 1934. In 1935 Lagonda won Le Mans with a six-cylinder 4½-litre Meadows-engined car. Built by Rapier Cars Ltd. from 1935-1940, the Rapier was available in supercharged form from 1936.

cash-flow. A receiver was appointed in 1935.

The company was bought by solicitor Alan Good for £67,000, just beating Rolls-Royce. The new company was called Lagonda Motors (Staines) Ltd. and the first move was to drop the Rapier.

Lagonda's designer was W. O. Bentley and his influence was first seen in the 4½-litre LG45, a modified M45, which was later improved by fitting a Meadows engine.

Bentley and his team unveiled the 2½-litre post-war Lagonda in September 1945. It had a twin-overhead-cam six-cylinder engine and cruciform chassis. But the Lagonda company never built it.

Tractor manufacturer David Brown bought Lagonda in 1947 for £52,500 and formed Aston Martin Lagonda.

The 2½-litre Lagonda went into production in 1949 and was replaced by the three-litre, made until 1958.

There have been three revivals of the Lagonda name, the current model being the Williams Towns-designed V8 saloon, and the marque's recent history is covered in the Aston Martin section.

Above: 1936 M45 2/4 Roadster

1937 Lagonda Rapide LG45. Capable of over 160km/h (100mph), the Rapide was powered by a 4467cc six-cylinder Meadows engine originally used by Invicta cars. With cross-flow cylinder head and other modifications it developed 150bhp.

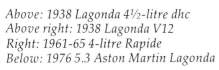

Above: 1938 Lagonda 4½-litre dhc
Above right: 1938 Lagonda V12
Right: 1961-65 4-litre Rapide
Below: 1976 5.3 Aston Martin Lagonda

Lamborghini

Italy
1947 to date

The legendary Lamborghini car grew from unlikely beginnings. Ferrucio Lamborghini was born in 1916 in Ferrara, north of Bologna, Italy, and gained technical knowledge of machinery working on a farm.

His knowledge was furthered by war-time service in the Italian air force and he later formed a business converting surplus military vehicles for agricultural use.

He loved fast cars, however, and modified a Fiat Topolino in 1947, racing it in the 1948 Mille Miglia.

Lamborghini Trattici was formed in 1949, building purpose-made tractors, and over ten a day were being built by 1959.

The business was expanded with the manufacture of domestic and industrial heating and air-conditioning systems, the healthy profits from which allowed Lamborghini a long-held ambition in 1963 – to build what he considered the ultimate car. Automobili Ferrucio Lamborghini SpA. was founded and a factory built at Sant'Agata Bolognese, between Modena and Bologna.

The new company's first car – the 3.5-litre V12 350GTV – was built at the tractor works, however, while construction was being finished at the car factory. It was exhibited at the Turin Show in 1963 and went into production in 1964 with a

Above: 1964 Lamborghini 350GT V12   *Below: 1967 400GT 2+2 3929cc 320bhp V12*

Below: 1967 3929cc Miura P400

slightly detuned engine.

Lamborghini had almost everything made at the Sant'Agata factory except the ZF five-speed gearbox. By 1964, however, the company was making its own final drives and gearboxes (with the unusual refinement of synchromesh on reverse gear) and 250 GTVs were being built every year.

The Miura P400 was launched at Turin in November 1965 and was joined the following year by the superb four-litre 400GT, a mid-engined coupé with more than a passing similarity to the Ford GT40. Lamborghini could now rightly

Above: 1971 Countach prototype   *Below: 1972 Espada 400GT*

Below: 1966 Lamborghini Miura P400, named after a breed of Spanish fighting bulls. With independent suspension and disc brakes all round, this five-speed mid-engined 4-litre V12 produced 350bhp at 7000rpm.

claim to be a challenger to Ferrari.

The Marzal prototype was first shown in 1967, with a two-litre six-cylinder engine derived from the V12. It never made production but paved the way for the four-seater V12-engined Espada. That was launched in 1968 and later joined by the 2+2 Islero, which was replaced by the Jarama in 1970.

The 2½-litre V8 Urraco represented Lamborghini's attempt to enter the small-sports-car market in 1971, but it lacked the character of his other cars.

Lamborghini had named the Miura after a fighting bull – his birth sign was Taurus, the bull. He chose its successor's name with equal care and the Countach – local dialect for something like 'that's it' – appeared in 1973. And it certainly was 'it', a sensationally fast car with equally sensational looks. Its mid-mounted V12 powerplant started out at four-litres, growing to five-litres in 1982.

Ferrucio Lamborghini decided to retire after a major slump in the Italian

Right: 1972 Urraco P250 2463cc V8
Below: 1974 Espada 3 3929cc V12

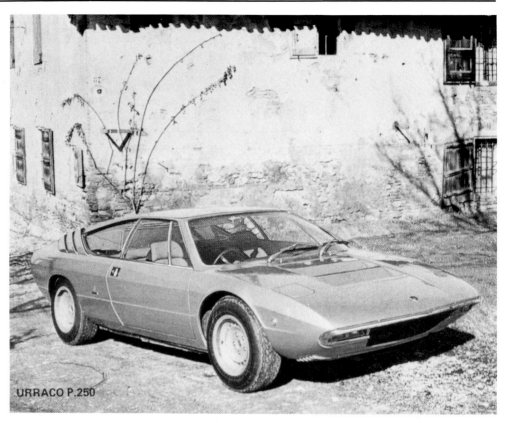

URRACO P.250

Above: 1974 Jarama 'S' 2+2 V12

agricultural industry, and in 1972 he sold control of the company to Georges-Henri Rosetti, a Swiss whose family had made a fortune in the clockmaking industry but who wanted to diversify because of competition from Japanese products.

Rosetti later sold part of his holding to a property-developer friend called Leimer. The company was then hit by general unrest in Italian industry and also by a failed deal under which Lamborghini would have built B.M.W. M1 sports cars.

The company later became the property of Hungarian-born American Zoltan Reti and he eventually put it into receivership.

Below: Lamborghini Countach, regarded by many as the ultimate road car. First seen in prototype form in the early 1970s, the Bertone-styled mid-engined V12 was made from 1973, grew wider wheel arches in 1978 and four-valve heads in 1985.

It was bought at auction by the Mimram family of Switzerland in June 1981.

The following year the 3.5-litre V8 Jalpa was launched, and early in 1985 a four-valve-per-cylinder Countach was announced, its V12 now boasting 5.2-litres and 455bhp. The company was later taken over by Chrysler and continues to produce the off-road LM002 vehicle and the Countach successor, the 492bhp 5.7-litre Diablo.

Above: 1986 Lamborghini Jalpa 3500

Above: 1981 Countach LP400S

Below: 1988 5167cc Countach

There are ambitious plans to increase production at Sant' Agata from the 350 cars per year of 1989 to 2,500 per year by 1994. Some 80 per cent of this output will be accounted for by the Jalpa replacement. Lamborghini himself returned to farming and he became a wine producer. One wine he offers is called, appropriately enough, 'Bulls' Blood'.

Above: LM002 455hp V12 off-roader

The Lamborghini Jalpa was launched in 1981 with a 3484cc V8 engine and a claimed top speed of 236km/h (147mph). This mid-engined Targa top supercar was destined for a short lifespan.

As with the Countach, the Diablo was due to have a long production run and the Lamborghini seemed stable in Chrysler's hands after it bought the company in 1987.

A year after its 1990 launch, a new model was offered alongside the standard car. The VT had four-wheel-drive, which was to put it directly into competition with Bugatti's EB110. Although grip was enhanced, it lacked the steering feel of the standard rear-wheel-drive model.

Lamborghini still had more tricks up its sleeves. In 1993, following a takeover by MegaTech in Bermuda, the Roadster was revealed. With no drop in power from the standard car's 492bhp and a negligible drop in performance, it became the fastest open-top production car in the world when it finally went into production in 1995.

1993 also marked the 30th anniversary of the creation of the company, so a special 525bhp Diablo was launched and later a new lightweight model, the SV. The 500bhp SV was widely regarded as the best driver's

Above: 1997 Diablo Roadster *Below: The fastest production convertible on earth*

car in the Diablo range and was only surpassed by the rare SVR with an extra 44bhp.
By 1997, the Diablo SVR was the only
supercar surviving that could compete with
McLaren's world-beating F1.

*Above: The stripped-out SV was the ultimate
Diablo evolution*

Right: The four-wheel-drive Diablo VT

*Below: This cutaway of the Diablo shows the
mid-mounted V12 engine, whose origins date
back to Lamborghini's first V12. This is the
four-wheel-drive VT model*

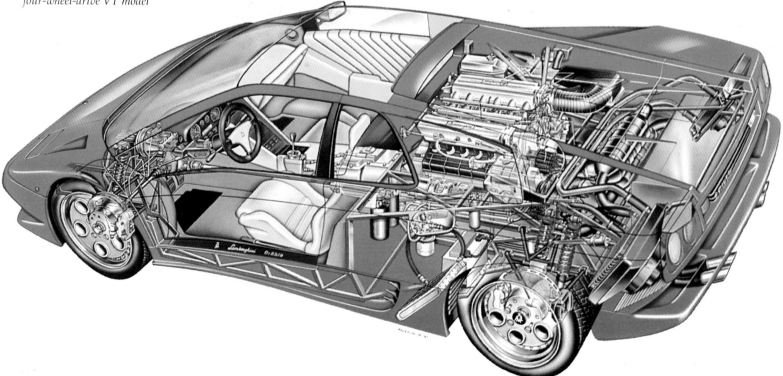

Lanchester

Great Britain
1895-1956

The first car produced by Frederick William Lanchester in 1895 was remarkable in that it was not a copy of a foreign model, nor was it an adaptation of a horse-drawn carriage, but a brilliant original design. Further prototypes followed and in late 1899 he founded the Lanchester Gas Engine Co., together with his two brothers George and Frank, who between them handled sales and publicity.

Six cars were produced by the factory in Sparkbrook, Birmingham, the year after, but cash-flow was always a problem. In 1904, just when the company was designing a new four-cylinder engine and the order books were full, it went bankrupt. George then took over the reformed Lanchester Motor Co. Ltd. from his brother Frederick, who eventually

resigned in 1913 and had no further connection with the company.

Lanchesters of that period were very distinctive, almost bonnetless with the engine mounted between the driver and

Above: 1897 8hp Lanchester two-cylinder

front-seat passenger. They also featured old-fashioned side-mounted tiller steering until 1911, when it was decided to make

Below: 1908 2470cc four-cylinder ohv three-speed 20hp Lanchester with tiller steering. The chassis design incorporated a fuel tank in its main crossmember. Good for 80km/h (50mph) it won a Gold Medal in the R.A.C.'s 1907 Vapour Emission Trials.

Above: 1902 Lanchester 8/12hp Tonneau
Below: 1908 two cylinder 12hp Lanchester

Above: 1922 40hp Sports Tourer
Below: 1923 6178cc six-cylinder Forty

Above: 1928 21hp short chassis tourer

the cars more conventional. They were extremely comfortable, and were owned by the likes of Rudyard Kipling, George Bernard Shaw and several Indian princes.

After making armoured cars during World War I, the company went into the luxury-car market with the 6.2-litre

Right: 1936 4½-litre (Vanden Plas body)
Below: 1913 38hp Torpedo Tourer
Below right: 1956 1.6-litre Sprite

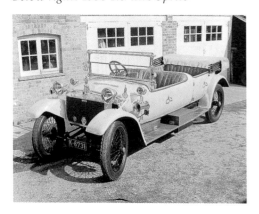

Sporting Forty, which lasted until 1929 and was given Royal patronage, but by 1931 financial troubles had struck again. The directors were forced to merge with Daimler, who wanted access to a cheaper market, and move the works to Coventry.

Frederick Lanchester continued successfully designing mechanical and electrical inventions until his death in 1946. George left the company in 1936 to join Alvis and died in 1970, ten years after his brother Frank.

Following World War II, many of the company's later cars were essentially low-price Daimlers with Lanchester radiator grilles. Two exceptions were the expensive Dauphin saloon, and an original design – the Sprite – which failed to enter production. By 1956 the once-great and respected Lanchester name had disappeared.

Lancia

Italy
1906 to date

One of Italy's oldest car manufacturers, Lancia was started in 1906. Bold and innovative, the company quickly gained a reputation for producing outstanding cars such as the 1922 Lambda and, much later, the 1972 Stratos.

Along the way the flashes of genius were tempered by some erratic performances in the field of manufacture, the terrible rust problems on the 1970s Beta range, for example, severely damaging the company's reputation.

The man behind the name was Vincenzo Lancia who was born in 1881 in Fobello, about 100 kilometres (60 miles) from Turin where his father Giuseppe based his canning business.

From an early age Vincenzo showed a mechanical aptitude and a capability for figures, so his father decided that he should study book-keeping. This led to an appointment as book-keeper for Giovanni Ceirano, importer for British Rudge bicycles.

Ceirano rented the ground floor of the Lancia family's Turin home and with engineer Aristide Faccioli had started producing his own bicycles and Welleyes car.

Young Lancia became totally absorbed in the mechanical side of the business and he had been with Ceirano for only a short period when the then recently formed F.I.A.T. made a bid for the new company.

Now 18, Vincenzo found himself appointed chief inspector for F.I.A.T. in Corso Dante and got on well with the company's secretary Giovanni Agnelli. When F.I.A.T. decided it wanted to go racing to promote its cars, Lancia was offered a drive and at Padua on 1 July 1900 he won his first race in class in a 6hp F.I.A.T. with a colleague from his Ceirano days – Felice Nazzaro – runner-up in a similar twin-cylinder model.

Regularly racing from then on, Lancia won the Coppa Florio in 1904, and finished eighth in the Gordon Bennett Cup

that year. Travelling to America for the 1905 Vanderbilt Cup races he set fastest lap and finished fourth after colliding with another car.

The following year saw him finish fifth in the first French Grand Prix, second in the Vanderbilt Cup giving F.I.A.T. a one-two, and he then went on to win the Coppa d'Oro in Milan.

Now 25 and a famous name in the

motoring world, Lancia decided to set up his own business after the 1906 racing season with fellow F.I.A.T. employee Claudio Fogolin who was to take care of sales and administration.

Their first car was ready by September 1907 – the 12hp Tipo 51 which actually

Above: 1908 Alfa 2543cc side valve
Below: 1909 Beta four-cylinder 3-litre

gave 24bhp at 1,450rpm from a 2543cc sidevalve engine.

The following year they built the six-cylinder 3815cc Dialpha. Only 23 were made, however, as the four-cylinder car was more popular and achieved 108 sales by the time production ceased in 1909.

In 1911 Lancia moved to much larger premises within Turin including room for expansion. There the 20–30hp 4080cc Delta was introduced and the overhead-cam 5030cc Eta.

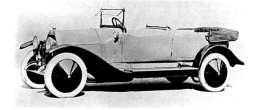

Above: 1913 Theta 4940cc

In 1918 came a 45-degree V8 and 30-degree V12 designs. The following year's V12 was tightened to a 22-degree angle allowing a one-piece cast block and featuring a single overhead camshaft. It was all very clever, but the car for which it was intended never went into production.

Below: 1913 Lancia Theta sold 1,696 examples. The 4940cc engine was already being used in Lancia IZ commercial vehicles and the unit was put to varied use during World War 1. The Theta engine was updated for use in the 1919 Kappa.

Having already displayed considerable ingenuity Lancia proved to the automotive world that there was plenty more to come. He had already patented a design for a car without a traditional chassis, his thoughts having been inspired by the hull of a ship. As well as a light and strong unit he also wanted independent front suspension. This was achieved in the shape of the 1922 2120cc V4 Lambda which was later improved with front-wheel braking and a rear-axle differential.

Above left: 1919 Kappa
Left: 1921 Dikappa produced 87bhp
Below: 1922 Trikappa 4594cc 98bhp V8

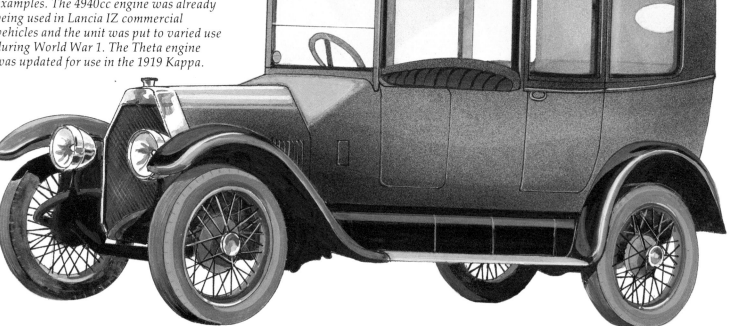

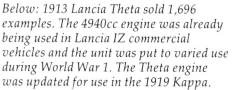

Above: 1929 3960cc V8 Dilambda Coupé

Lancia set up a factory in France which alone produced 2,500 examples. Total sales exceeded 15,000. A separate-chassis version was later produced to satisfy the coachbuilding trade and the car was made

Above: 1923 2120cc V4 Lambda
Right: 1931 2972cc V8 Astura

The car was capable of almost 112km/h (70mph), and was extremely roomy. No less than 12,530 were built in nine series during the model's 1922–31 lifespan.

Lancia then decided to tempt wealthier customers with the 1929 Dilambda with a 3960cc 24-degree V8. Built in three series up to 1932, 1,686 were made.

The Depression of the 1930s caused Lancia to look to an inexpensive model. At the 1932 Paris Motor Show he unveiled his unit-construction 18-degree 1194cc V4 Augusta. It became a best seller and

Below: The 1922 Lancia Lambda greatly enhanced Lancia's reputation, thanks to unit construction and independent pillar front suspension. The 13-degree 2120cc V4 engine was single ohc giving 49bhp at 3,250rpm.

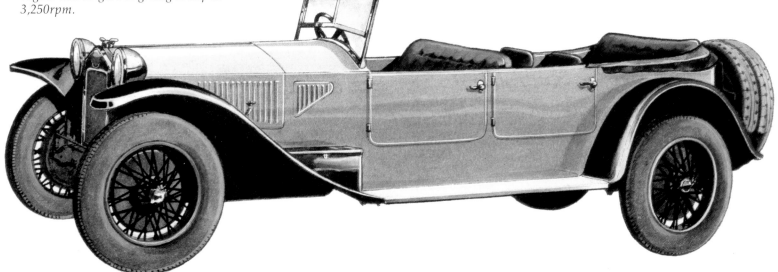

Above: 1931 Artena 1924cc V4
Right: 1933 1194cc V4 Augusta
Below: 1949 five-speed version of Ardea

until 1937 when, along with the Astura, it was phased out.

The new blade in Lancia's armoury came in the shape of the aerodynamically styled Aprilia. With a 1351cc V4 engine and low overall weight, it featured independent suspension all round and inboard rear drum brakes. Introduced to the public in 1937 it was capable of almost 128km/h (80mph) and displayed excellent roadholding for its time. Production of the new car coincided with Lancia's death in February 1937 following illness. He was 55. His wife Adèle took over as president of the company, aided by Manlio Gracco.

Arturo Lancia, a cousin of the late Vincenzo became the company's general manager in 1944, by which time the factory had moved to Bolzano following shelling of the Turin factory. After the war the Turin factory was rebuilt and Bolzano used for commercial-vehicle production.

In 1945 manufacture of the Aprilia and Ardea resumed. By 1949 23,717 Aprilias had been built. Both models were upgraded to 12-volt electrics and the Ardea received a five-speed gearbox in 1948. It was claimed to be the world's first production car so equipped. When Ardea production ceased in 1953, over 22,000 had been built.

Meanwhile a new Lancia star had emerged from the wings, the Aurelia of 1950. Masterminded by Lancia's son Gianni, who had taken command of the company in 1948, the B10 was the first production car in the world to boast a V6 engine. It also featured a Vittorio Jano-designed four-speed gearbox incorporated in the rear axle. Semi-trailing arm independent rear suspension was another world first for the unit-construction Aurelia.

Platform-chassis versions were also available for coach builders, and Pininfarina's coupé version set a trend for Gran Turismo cars featuring what was effectively a sporting car with saloon-car comfort. The GT won the 1952 Targa Florio and the GT2500 version the 1954 Monte Carlo Rally, the same year that saw the introduction of the very pretty Pininfarina Spyder version.

The V4 Appia arrived in 1953 and lasted for ten years, meanwhile Lancia was doing well in sports-car racing, moving into Formula One in 1954 with a twin-cam 260bhp V8 of 2489cc. By this time, however, Lancia was on shaky financial ground and negotiations commenced with Fiat and Ferrari. Under an agreement Lancia passed most of its D50 F1 cars to Ferrari who modified the design and won five Grands Prix in 1956.

Above: 1955 Aurelia B20 Coupé

Cement manufacturer Carlo Pesenti had taken control of Lancia in 1955. He appointed Professor Antonio Fessia as

Above: 1956 V6 Aurelia Spyder

technical head and the result was the Flaminia shown at Geneva in 1956. A luxury saloon, it was V6-powered but sold poorly and was discontinued in 1965.

Fessia had previously designed a front-wheel-drive car and pursued his conviction for this system with the Flavia, Lancia's and Italy's first front-wheel-drive car. Production of the 1500cc flat-four began in 1961 and it paved the way for Lancia's best selling Fulvia. Over 300,000 examples were sold of this small front-wheel-drive car which employed a V4 engine in various sizes starting with the

1951-7 Lancia Aurelia B20 Gran Turismo Coupé styled by Pininfarina set a trend for 'fastback' cars. The 1754cc 60-degree V6 transmitted its 56bhp to a four-speed gearbox in the rear axle. A 2.5-litre version won the 1954 Monte Carlo Rally.

Above: 1956 Flaminia Coupé 2458cc V6

1091cc unit of 1963.

A second-series coupé version was released in 1969, the year Lancia and its considerable debts were taken over by Fiat. With the Fulvia, Lancia had great success in rallying and this success was continued with the incredible-looking Stratos rally car of 1972. Styled by Bertone and powered by a 2.4-litre Ferrari Dino V6, the car won the world rally

Above: 1963 front-wheel-drive V4 Fulvia

Above right: 1971 1991cc Lancia 2000
Below right: 1972 front-wheel-drive Beta
Below: 1964 V6 Flaminia convertible

championships in 1974, 1975 and 1976.

The Beta range was introduced in 1972 powered by Fiat twin-cam four-cylinder engines of 1438cc driving the front wheels. A two-litre mid-engined version, the Beta Monte Carlo, was introduced in 1975 along with the Gamma powered by a 2484cc flat-four engine developed by Lancia.

The company's first small hatchback was the Delta of 1980. Actually made by Fiat, it was voted Car of the Year.

Above: 1976 2-litre Monte Carlo

Below: 1976 2.5-litre Gamma saloon

Two views of the 1976 four-cylinder and 2500 Gamma Coupé

1971 Lancia Fulvia Coupé 2+2. Designed by Pietro Castagnero it was first seen at the 1965 Turin Show with a 1216cc V4 power unit. A 1600cc version won the 1972 Monte Carlo Rally and World Rally championship.

Below: 1974 Stratos. With mid-mounted 1600cc HF engine, it was first shown in 1970 and produced in 1972. Later fitted with a dohc 190bhp Ferrari Dino V6 engine, it went on to claim five Monte Carlo Rally wins.

Above: 1976 Lancia Stratos

The 1995cc single-overhead-camshaft Thema replaced the Gamma in 1985. A turbocharged version and 2849cc V6 followed, resources for this car being shared between Lancia, Fiat, Saab and Alfa Romeo. Later Ferrari provided the three-litre 32-valve V8 engine for the 8.32 Thema of 1986.

In the world of hot hatchbacks none came hotter than the turbocharged HF Delta four-wheel-drive car, competition versions of which won the 1983, 1987, 1988 and 1989 world rally championships.

The tiny Y10 with Fiat's 999cc 'F.I.R.E.' engine was introduced in 1985. It is marketed in its home market as an Autobianchi.

Though part of a large conglomerate the Lancia name forges onward particularly thanks to the Delta which has taken Lancia to its seventh world rally championship, the best record of any manufacturer in this sport.

Above: 1977 Lancia Beta Coupé

Below: 1988 Delta HF 4wd Rally king

Above: 1982 Lancia Trevi 1585/1995cc

Above: 1985 999cc Y10 hatchback

Above: 1985 1049cc turbocharged Y10

Above: 1986 Lancia Prisma LX

Below: 1987 Ferrari-powered Thema 8.32

Although sales were few and far between during the recession (in fact the company had to stop exporting to Britain in 1994), Lancia survived and started to re-establish itself as Fiat's luxury car wing. The Delta gained four-wheel-drive later in life and soon proved itself to be an unbeatable rally car, in this Integrale form, with its lively turbocharged engine and fantastic grip. It was good enough to knock the Audi Quattro from the winner's podium. Initially it competed in Group B rallying with a 500bhp mid-engined version, but when Group B was banned at the end of 1986, a more conventional, front-engined car took over. The Delta Integrale, in various evolutions, completely dominated the World Rally Championship, winning it every year from 1987 to 1992.

The road version of the Delta was updated in 1993 with new smoother bodywork and engines with power outputs ranging from a 103bhp 1.6-litre to a 186bhp turbocharged 2.0-litre. A three-door version, designated HPE, was launched in 1995. Lancia never campaigned the new Delta as a rally car.

The Y10 was replaced by the stylish Y, although the Y10 continued to sell in some markets badged as an Autobianchi. The Y's clean, cropped look was very modern and adventurous, like most cars coming from the Fiat Group's design studios in the 1990s.

The Dedra, launched in 1989 to replace the Prisma of 1983, was of rather conventional design in comparison to the

Above: 1997 Lancia Y

Below: Lancia Kappa estate

Left: New Lancia Delta

Below: Lancia Dedra Station Wagon

rest of Lancia's late-1990s range. A simple three-box saloon, it was still a relatively successful seller.

The innovative Kappa saloon, which was first revealed to the public in 1994, was joined in 1996 by an estate version and a stunning two-door coupé. The Coupé's crisp styling bore a resemblance to the pretty, but ill-fated Lancia Gamma of the 1970s.

Z was Lancia's version of the PSA/Fiat MPV people carrier.

Top left: Lancia Kappa saloon

Above: Lancia Z

Left: Lancia Dedra saloon

Below: Lancia Kappa Coupé

Laurin-Klement/ Skoda

Czechoslovakia 1906 to date

Skoda, Czechoslovakia's best-known motor manufacturer, began life very humbly in the early 1890s when Vaclav Klement left his bookshop and joined mechanic Vaclav Laurin to form a bicycle-repair business in Mlada Boleslav in norther Czechoslovakia (then part of the Austro-Hungarian Empire). In 1898 they began to produce what is acknowledged to be the world's first true motor-cycle, and in 1905 unveiled their first motor car, the Model A Voiturette. It had a four-stroke twin-cylinder engine developing 7hp, a three-speed gearbox with reverse and a top speed of 48km/h (30mph).

During the following years new models were introduced including the Ds and Es with four-cylinder engines, the type B-2 motor cab and, finally, what was probably their greatest pre-World War I model, the Type FF with a 4854cc eight-cylinder engine developing 40bhp.

The company also built buses and lorries, had outlets worldwide, and gained many racing and rallying successes under the leadership of Otto Hyeronymus, an outstanding designer and experienced racing driver who joined the company in 1908.

In 1925 Laurin and Klement were taken over by Akciova Spolecnot, a manufacturer of heavy machinery and armaments, and all future cars carried the Skoda name and emblem. From 1924 to 1930 Skoda had been building Hispano-Suiza cars under licence but it was in 1928 that the first new models rolled off the production line with four-, six- and eight-cylinder engines ranging in capacity from 1944cc to 3880cc. One of the best-selling cars of this era was the Type 420 launched in 1933, with rear swing half-axles and a centre tubular chassis – a design which was to be used over the next 30 years.

The following year the 420 was given a face-lift to produce the very successful Popular, Skoda's first small family car,

Above: 1906 Type B Laurin-Klement

Below: 1907 Type F Landau Laurin-Klement

Right: Skoda factory in 1930
Below: 1929 Type 422 Skoda

with a 903cc (later 995cc) engine developing 18bhp, and whose worldwide sales established Skoda in the international market. The other popular cars of the time were the 1165cc (later 1380cc) Rapid and the six-cylinder 2941cc Superb. During this period Skoda kept up its interest in rallying, performing well in several long-distance events including the Monte Carlo Rally.

An important change occurred in 1938 when overhead-valve engines were developed for the Popular (1089cc), the Rapid (1558cc) and the Superb (3140cc), and during this period Skoda reached its highest pre-war production figure of 6,371 cars a year.

In 1952 the Skoda 1200 was launched as a roomy four-door saloon with a 1221cc engine, followed some three years later by the similarly-powered Octavia and Felicia. From 1964 onwards, following the building of a huge new works, Skoda

Top: 1965 Skoda Kombi Estate
Above: 1969 1000 MB De Luxe Mk II
Above left: 1950 1089cc roadster

concentrated mainly on rear-engined cars, the first being the 1000 MB (MB for Mlada Boleslav) a chassisless monocoque design with a 988cc 40bhp engine, followed by the 1100 MB with the slightly larger 1107cc engine.

Below: 1982 Skoda 120 Rapid Coupé with rear mounted 1174cc four-speed engine unit, rack and pinion steering, independent suspension, servo assisted front disc brakes, alloy wheels, halogen headlamps, front air dam and rear spoiler.

Production continued through the 1970s with the S100, 110, and 120 rear-engined models of 988cc to 1147cc capacities, with the Estelle series becoming firm favourites as well as being among the cheapest cars in western Europe. The Estelle is still in production in 1989, although Skoda did finally enter the front-wheel-drive market with its long-awaited Favorit, launched in 1988 with a 1289cc all-aluminium engine and compact Bertone-designed body, thus gradually bringing to an end the 40-year reign of the rear-engined Skodas.

Below: 1977 Skoda Super Estelle 120L

Right: 1987 Skoda 130GL 1289cc

Below: 1984 Skoda 105GL four-door saloon with 1046cc ohv four-cylinder rear-mounted engine.

Above: Cabriolet Rapid introduced 1984

Below: 1989 fwd Favorit 1.3 GLX

With the introduction of the new Favorit, things looked set to change at Skoda. It was a radical departure from previous cars, distinctly more modern and consequently attracting new buyers. It also drew the attention of Volkswagen. In the early 1990s. Volkswagen bought Skoda and set about further improving the company's dowdy, downmarket image as well as bringing build quality up to Volkswagen standards.

In 1994, Volkswagen updated the Bertone styling, renaming the car Felicia. It was a westernized Skoda, with smoother, more modern lines, better build quality; somehow it was just a little bit more of a Volkswagen. The Felicia was the car that really showed the world that Skoda could make good and competitive cars, and was a completely different company to the one which had for so long been the butt of so many jokes.

To broaden the range, Skoda launched the Octavia in 1996. The name was old but the car was all new. It was available with 1.6-, 1.8- or 1.9-litre diesel engines. The base engine came from the Felicia, the more powerful 1.6 and 1.9 diesel from Volkswagen, and the 1.8 was an all-new 20-valve design, pushing out 125bhp.

Volkswagen's help was invaluable to Skoda, and the company's image had come a long way by the late 1990s, but there was

still a way to go before the company could really compete with western European companies.

Above: The Felicia showed what Skoda could do with Volkswagen's help

Below: 1997 Skoda Octavia

Above: The Octavia had VW family styling

Below: Felicia Estate was a useful load carrier

Lea-Francis

Great Britain 1904 to date

Though often seen by enthusiasts as a marque that embodies the best of British sporting tradition, the fact is that Lea-Francis never set out to be a company that anything at all to do with motor racing.

Instead, their story is one of haphazardly flitting between ideas, some bad and some good, and their successes never seemed to be any more part of a premeditated plan than their failures.

R. H. Lea and G. J. Francis were both involved in the bicycle industry when they started the firm in 1895 in Coventry. And indeed bicycles were their first products. Motor-cycles also came from the company a little later, and were to continue for some time – in fact, considerably after World War I. However, they produced a car in 1904 which did not meet with a terribly enthusiastic reception, and was discontinued after only two years, only two ever sold.

In 1922, though, they returned to four wheels, and though interest was still not exactly fanatical, they persevered. Links were forged with the Vulcan company, an established car maker of the time, and after a few false starts with odd or otherwise unpalatable models, they acquired the rights to use the comparatively powerful Meadows engine in their rather lumpy cars.

However, as they gained confidence the firm tried the 1500cc Meadows powerplant in its 'Ten' model, and the combination of a light chassis and a sporting engine gave it performance well beyond the reach of most of its rivals. In the 1924 R.A.C. Six Days Small Car Trials, held in Wales, it out-climbed everything and a motor sport reputation was born.

The Meadows engine proved tuneable and reliable, and although it was used by other British sports-car makers it still remained part and parcel of the Lea-Francis legend. And it set the tone for their future products, too. Though staid

Below: A 1925 Lea-Francis four-seater

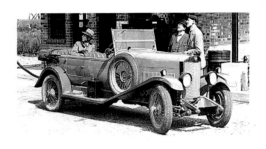

Above: The Vulcan-built LFS 14/40
Below: The 1928 'Brooklands' model

saloons were still available, the sportier end of the firm's range soon sprouted such innovatory stuff as centre-lock wire wheels, front-wheel brakes and eventually supercharging, which added another dimension to the potency of the product and made the 'Hyper' model one of the most sought-after sporting cars of the late 1920s, with many racing wins to its credit.

Abortive experiments with in-house

Below: The Hyper Sports S-Type was one of the company's finest products, bringing many competition successes and much publicity to the Lea-Francis name. Everything, in fact, but profit.

Above: 1939 Avon-bodied coupé
Below: One of the last, a 1952 saloon

Above: The 1929 TT Hyper

six-cylinder powerplants followed, which lasted several years before a useful engine, the so-called 'Ace of Spades', was developed and by 1930 the new engine was installed in a car and shown to the public. Unfortunately, despite the success of the marque in competition the company's misguided attempts to produce a luxury saloon had sent its finances spiralling downwards and it went into receivership the very same year. The company closed in 1935.

Two years later it returned, only to be confronted by the war, which resulted in crippling purchase tax, a terrible shortage of materials and threatening exhortations to export or else – not the ideal situation for a home-market-based company.

A lingering death was the inevitable result. By 1953 Lea-Francis had disappeared from the Motor Show, and by 1958 had even closed its service station. In 1960 the strangely styled Lynx, a Ford-engined effort, was launched unsuccessfully, and after a few oddities like bubble-cars and agricultural equipment, the company went down for the second time.

It reappeared in 1980 with little success, and has recently tried another expensive luxury car.

Below: The Jaguar-based 1980 version

Lexus

Japan
1988 to date

In 1988 and in order to break into the luxury car market, especially in the United States, Toyota created a new brand; the new company was called Lexus. The Lexus range was limited but the cars were loaded with almost every conceivable extra.

The mainstay of the range was the LS400. A large, five-seater saloon, the LS400 had smart, though slightly bland looks. In order to ensure good U.S. sales, a large (by Japanese or European standards) capacity V8 engine was used. Displacing nearly 4.0 litres and with two overhead camshafts per bank, the new all-alloy engine gave a healthy 264bhp by the late 1990s. Japanese build, quality and reliability, allied to transatlantic styling and without a recognizably Japanese brand name meant it was a great success,

especially in the States. It was also available in two-door coupé form.

To follow up on its success in America, Toyota created another Lexus designed for American tastes. The SC300 and SC400 coupé were launched in 1991. With either

Above: 1996 Lexus LS400

Below: Lexus GS300 Sport

the 3.0-litre straight six or the 4.0-litre V8 from the LS400, the sleek SCs were fast cars but they were by no means sporting. Ultimate luxury was still the main factor.

Lexus succeeded by building typically American cars, with Japanese principles and new technology. The result was an undoubtedly more competent car than was produced by any American manufacturer. However, Toyota forgot one important ingredient –

Top: 1995 Lexus SC400

Right: 1996 Lexus SC300

Below: 1996 Lexus LS450

character. By aiming for engineering excellence they had designed out whatever character, in looks or performance, that the car might have had.

The top-of-the-range Toyota Camry and Land Cruiser were sold in America bearing the Lexus badge, as was the Giugiaro-designed GS300. The GS300 was perhaps Lexus' best-looking offering, managing to look like a coupé despite being a four-door, five-seater vehicle. The bolder styling made it more desirable than the more expensive, but blander, top-of-the-range models.

Leyland

Great Britain
1920 to date

The name Leyland has, in one way or another, been linked with many of this century's famous car manufacturers.

Leyland was the Lancashire village where the Sumner family ran a blacksmith's forge and where the family experimented with steam-powered vehicles at the turn of the century.

They went on to make trucks, and Leyland Motors Ltd. was formed in 1907.

Henry Spurrier, one of the financial backers, decided the company should build a luxury car and the 7.3-litre Leyland Eight was introduced at the 1920 Olympia Motor Show.

The philosophy was simple – to build

Above: 1920 Leyland Eight show model

the world's finest car, with money being no object.

But only 18 were built as the company hit financial problems.

Leyland struggled and in 1923 had a £1

million deficit but, under new management, was back in profit by 1926, helped by sales of its trucks and buses.

Donald Stokes, who had joined the company as an apprentice in 1930, led a

Below: 1922 Leyland Eight Tourer

Above: 1925 Leyland Trojan 10hp Utility

Above: 1931 Leyland Trojan 10hp RE

successful export campaign after World War II and by 1954 Leyland was making £1 million a year.

With sales of commercials flourishing, Stokes decided to re-enter the car market, acquiring Standard Triumph in 1961, A.C.V. – which owned A.E.C., Thornycroft, Maudslay and Crossley – in 1962, and Rover in 1967.

Stokes became managing director in 1962 after Sir Henry Spurrier Jr., son of the original backer, suffered a serious illness.

Meanwhile, the British Motor Corporation was forming, with its main elements being Austin, Morris, M.G., Riley and Wolseley.

B.M.C. also acquired Jaguar, Daimler and Coventry-Climax in 1966 to become British Motor Holdings Ltd.

Leyland and British Motor Holdings combined to form the British Leyland Motor Corporation early in 1968, with Stokes as chief executive on a joint board.

The company was dogged with problems in the early 1970s including rising oil prices, industrial unrest, duplication of resources and falling demand.

A government report said that the corporation was destined for failure without a massive cash boost and B.M.C. was reorganized as British Leyland Ltd. in 1975.

Ostensibly it was a public company with the government holding 95.1 per cent of the shares.

New models were launched and old names such as Wolseley, Riley and Triumph disappeared.

The company was unwieldy and continued to have problems. Managing director Alex Park was replaced by Michael Edwardes in 1978 and he spent four years saving it from extinction.

He left in 1983 and the company was split into the Austin-Rover Group Ltd., Land-Rover Group, Leyland Vehicles Ltd. and Jaguar Cars. The latter was floated as a public company in 1984.

The name Leyland effectively no longer exists for car manufacture but continues with commercial vehicles.

Below: 1959 948cc Triumph Herald

Lincoln

U.S.A.
1920 to date

Henry Martyn Leland, the founder of Lincoln, began his working career with gun and munitions manufacturers. By 1890 he was a partner, along with his son Wilfred, in a machine-shop business, and gained an excellent reputation for precision engineering.

After associations with the original Henry Ford Company and Cadillac (the latter evolving from the former) and the production of Liberty V12 aero-engines during World War I, the Lelands' thoughts turned towards production of their own car. Consequently, they designed and built a beautifully engineered chassis powered by a 357-cubic inch (5850cc) V8, and announced a range of cars under the name of Lincoln in September 1920.

Unfortunately, Henry Leland, like Henry Ford, failed to appreciate the increasing significance of styling, and the new cars looked stodgy. This factor, combined with a recession in 1920, led to poor sales and ultimately to receivership in November 1921. The Lelands approached Henry Ford about him buying the company. Henry, it appears, was indifferent to the idea, but his son Edsel, who appreciated fine cars, was most enthusiastic. Consequently Ford bought Lincoln in February 1922 for U.S. $8 million.

Although there was nothing in writing, the Lelands thought they could stay on and run things their way, which naturally led to friction with the Fords. Matters

Above: 1925 5.8-litre V8
Below: 1928 6.3-litre

Above: 1927 Lincoln V8
Below: 1929 V8 Lincoln Sedan

came to a head on 13 June 1922 when Wilfred was ordered out of the plant and his father Henry resigned in protest. The Lelands were never to return.

Under Ford the L series, once restyled, sold profitably, remaining in production for ten years. The luxury V12 K series, introduced in 1931, suffered during the Depression, but lasted until 1939 when Edsel Ford conceived the Continental.

The gap between the Lincoln K and the basic Ford V8 line was vast so, in 1936, the intermediate Lincoln Zephyr was

launched, followed by the lower-priced Mercury marque in 1939.

Edsel Ford died in 1943, followed by Henry in 1947, and this marked a turning point for Lincoln. After the war, under the

Below: 1928 6.31-litre V8 luxury sedan. Horsepower was increased to 90 for 1930, and two years later a fabulous 150bhp V12 was added to the line with a choice of no less than 23 body types! The V8 model was dropped during 1933, V8 Lincolns reappearing in 1948.

Top: 1934 Convertible Roadster
Above: 1937 four-door Phaeton
Below: 1939 'Sunshine' Special

guidance of Henry Ford II, and the direct control of Benson Ford, Lincoln was groomed to increase its profitability and market share, the latter with some success

as sales quadrupled to 22 per cent of the luxury-car market between 1950 and 1953.

However, by the late 1950s Lincoln had lost direction – and sales. The problem was the lack of a coherent image. After World War II Lincoln had built a variety of cars, which had appealed to different segments of the market. Cadillac, it was concluded, had maintained a constant image, as its models always 'looked' like Cadillacs.

The saviour of Lincoln was the 1961 Continental, a very cleanly styled car which left the competition standing. From then on Lincoln slowly began to reinstate itself as a luxury-car maker, culminating with the instant success of the Continental Mark III, which sold 23,088 units during the 1969 model year.

By 1970 the Lincoln/Cadillac sales ratio was one to four, rising from one to three in 1971, as annual sales surpassed 100,000 cars for the first time. Lincoln now dominated the personal luxury-car market.

A slight disappointment, in terms of sales, was the 1977–80 Versailles, a comparatively small luxury sedan, which competed with the Cadillac Seville.

By 1979 Lincoln was offering a range of full-sized cars for the last time and, indeed, had this market to itself. To commemorate this Lincoln offered a

Below: Lincoln Continental 7.5-litre V8 four-door sedan luxury tourer with air conditioning. Over 5.5m (18ft) in length, this giant gave way to more compact designs in the mid-1980s.

'Collector Series' option on the Continental and Mark V models.

The 1980s saw poor sales initially, mostly due to economic recession, but as the decade progressed sales of the rationalized and fuel-efficient Lincoln models picked up, and the company consolidated its hold on the luxury-car market.

Top: 1950 Lincoln Cosmopolitan
Above: 1968 Continental
Below: 1988 Lincoln Mk VII LSC

Ford's prestige car division, Lincoln, continued to compete with Cadillac at the top of the scale of American cars.

The biggest news of the 1990s was the launch of the Lincoln Mark VIII in 1992. It had sleek ultra-modern styling and a powerful V8 engine as well as plenty of gadgets and unique features. One particularly unusual feature were the wing mirror-mounted floor lights which illuminated the ground under the doors. A double-skinned firewall in the engine bay helped keep engine noise to a minimum

The Lincoln Continental, updated in 1987, continued the great name's tradition. The 1997 model even came equipped with a satellite system to enable rescue or breakdown services to locate the car more easily.

The Lincoln Town Car was a machine from another age. Despite its rounded-off styling, the Town Car was just a huge lumbering V8 giant that looked like it belonged in the seventies rather than the nineties.

Like Mercury, Lincoln had its own version of the Ford Expedition 4x4. Of course,

Above: 1997 Lincoln Continental

Below: 1997 Lincoln Mark VIII

the Lincoln version, the Navigator, was about the most luxurious 4x4 on the market. It arrived a year later than the Mercury model and was launched in 1997.

Left: Rear-view of the 1997 Lincoln Mark VIII

Above: The Mark VIII's innovative and unique lighting system

Below: The 1997 Lincoln Town Car

Locomobile

U.S.A.
1899–1929

The Locomobile Company of America began life in Westboro, Massachusetts. The partners, A. L. Barber and J. B. Walker, produced their first vehicle in 1899, after buying the rights to the Stanley brothers' steam-powered designs. Shortly after this Walker left to start Mobile and Barber continued with Locomobile, moving to Bridgeport, Connecticut, in 1900. The two marques were remarkably similar in mechanics, differing only in bodywork.

The first model was also sold in England at this time by W. M. Letts, with some success. The following year A. L. Riker joined Locomobile as vice-president and chief engineer. Riker had begun with electric cars before producing petrol-engined Panhard-type designs. It was these Barber chose to replace his steam-driven vehicles, selling the old patents back to the Stanleys.

By 1905 the company were producing Mercedes-style cars aimed at the luxury market, and were also involved with racing. In 1908 George Robertson won the Vanderbilt Cup with a two-year-old Locomobile 'Old 16'. Five years later the company took the touring-car section of the Glidden Tour. Its most famous

Top: 1901 6hp Steamer twin cylinder
Right: 1916 six-cylinder Speedster
Below: 1900 Steam buggy
Below centre: 1901 Steam buggy
Far right: 1899-1903 Steamer Runabouts

road-going car was the 48, introduced in 1911, which was to last until 1929.

During World War I Locomobile made tank engines, staff cars and trucks. Locomobile had been producing commercials since 1912, which were badged as Rikers from 1916 until 1921 when they were phased out.

Financial problems led to the company joining the Emlen Hare's Motor Group in 1920, along with Crane-Simplex and Mercer. Two years later Locomobile's losses were running level with its assets and it was acquired by the William C. Durant empire, mainly to produce Flint cars.

Durant attempted to widen Locomobile's appeal with the cheaper Junior 8 range of 1925 which brought an increase in sales. It also lowered the tone of the marque which was unable to survive the onset of the Depression, closing in 1929.

Top: Post 1915 Model 48 Sportif
Above: c. 1915 Model 48 Gunboat Roadster

Below: 1925 Junior Eight with 3.25-litre overhead valve engine outsold larger models by eight to one, but against opposition such as Chrysler and General Motors it was expensive. The Depression finished the company.

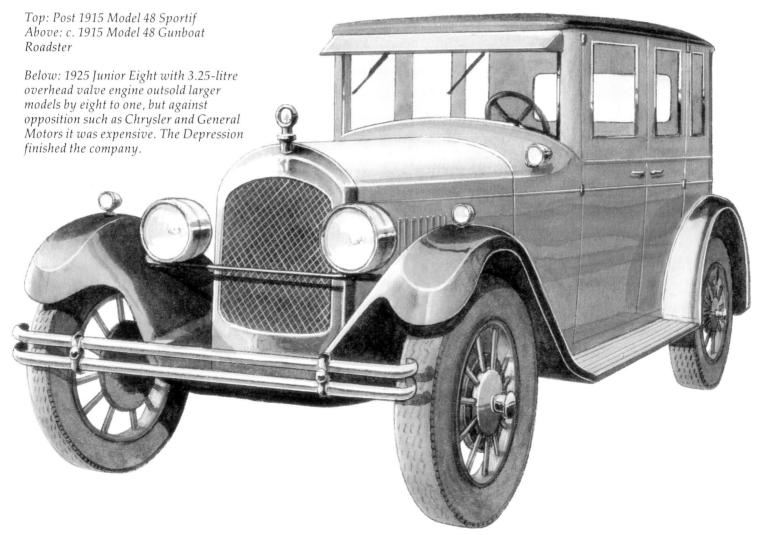

Lotus

Great Britain
1952 to date

The famous Lotus name stemmed from one man and his love of cars.

Anthony Colin Bruce Chapman was born in Richmond, Surrey, in 1928 and his first car was a 1937 Morris Eight Tourer – a Christmas gift from his parents in 1945.

He started making some extra pocket-money by buying and selling cars. But petrol rationing hit his business hard and in 1947 he decided to build a special based on a 1930 Austin Seven fabric-bodied saloon. It was completed in a lockup garage early in 1948 and used successfully in trials.

After finishing his national service with the R.A.F., Chapman worked as a constructional engineer with a London-based steel-erecting company, and later joined the British Aluminium Company as

Below: Colin Chapman and 1957 Elite

Above: Colin Chapman and Lotus 7

a development engineer.

Work started on the Mark 3 in January 1951. Chapman built one for himself and two for the brothers Michael and Nigel Allen, moving to their workshop in Wood Green, north London.

He was asked to build a Mark 4 and went into partnership with Michael Allen

to form the Lotus Engineering Co. on 1 January 1952, moving into an old stable at Hornsey, north London. The Mark 4 was highly significant for the company – it was the first Lotus with a purpose-built spaceframe chassis (as opposed to a modified Austin frame) and it was designed for road use as well as competition.

The Mark 5 was never built but its basic design was used for the Mark 6 which had a Ford Consul engine.

The company became Lotus Engineer-

Below: 1966 Lotus Ford Cortina

1957 Motor Show and it was made by an offshoot company, Lotus Components Ltd. The car was mainly offered in kit-form to take advantage of British tax exemptions.

It was the success of the 7 which really established the Lotus name and Chapman moved to larger premises at Cheshunt, Hertfordshire, in June 1959, becoming Lotus Cars Ltd. and Lotus Components Ltd.

Most of his cars were for racing and the Mark 9, with a Coventry-Climax engine, made Lotus's Le Mans debut. The first Lotus single-seater came in 1957 – the Lotus 12 for Formula 2 events – and the 16 was the first Formula 1 car.

Stirling Moss took Lotus to its first Grand Prix win in 1960 in Rob Walker's privately entered Climax-engined 18. It was to be followed by many world-class wins.

Above left: 1951 Lotus Mk 3

Below: 1958 Lotus Mk 16

ing in February 1952. Allen left and Chapman's girlfriend Hazel Williams became the other director. She lent the company £25 – its total working capital. Chapman was still working for British Aluminium yet managed to make one car a fortnight.

There was to be no Mark 7 as such – although this designation was, of course, later allocated to a much more famous car – and work began on the Mark 8 in January 1954. Chapman married Hazel the following October and the next year, 1956, exhibited at the Motor Show for the first time.

Lotus's racing department was set up in 1957, by which time Chapman had gained a good reputation with Grand Prix teams such as B.R.M. and Vanwall for whom he designed suspension and chassis.

He launched the Lotus 7 at the October

1958 Lotus 7, a spartan two-seater which made the marque into a legend. Versions included the F-model with 1172cc 36bhp Ford four-cylinder engine. The A-model accepted B.M.C.'s A-series four-cylinder unit.

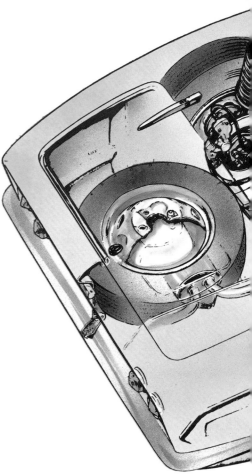

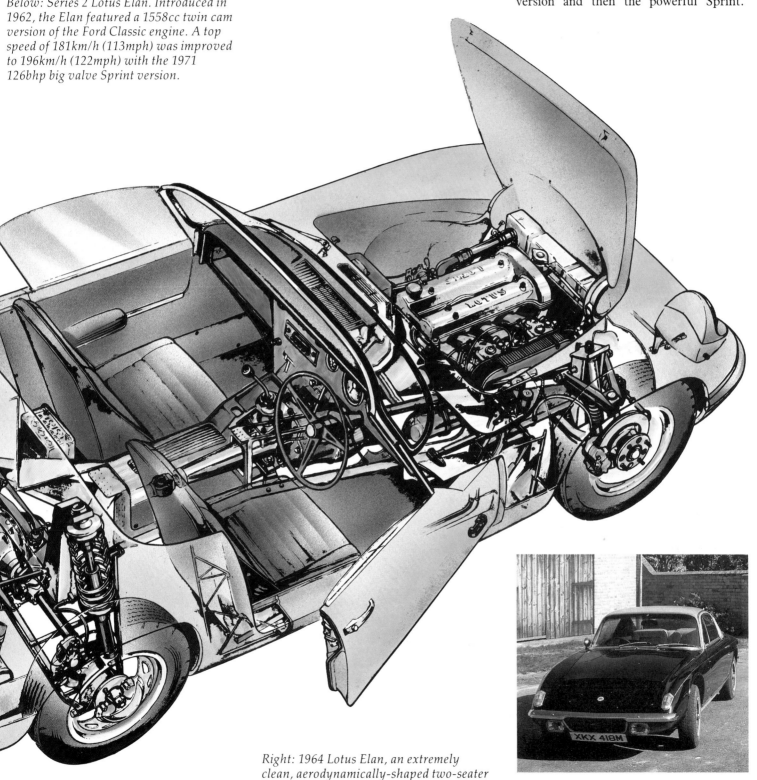

Left: 1968 Lotus Elan S4
Below left: 1973 Elan Coupé

Below: Series 2 Lotus Elan. Introduced in 1962, the Elan featured a 1558cc twin cam version of the Ford Classic engine. A top speed of 181km/h (113mph) was improved to 196km/h (122mph) with the 1971 126bhp big valve Sprint version.

Meanwhile, Chapman continued with his road cars and about 1,000 glassfibre Elites had been built by March 1964. The famous Elan was introduced in 1962, using a Ford-based twin-cam engine, and it was later joined by a fixed-head coupé, a Plus 2 version and then the powerful Sprint.

Right: 1964 Lotus Elan, an extremely clean, aerodynamically-shaped two-seater

The mid-engined Europa came in 1966 and, with its cars becoming more sophisticated, Lotus moved to a large factory at Hethel, near Norwich, and even began building its own engines.

Lotus became a public company in October 1968 with most of the ordinary shares remaining with the Chapman family, and from January 1969 Group Lotus Car Companies Ltd. was the holding company for the subsidiaries such as Lotus Cars and Lotus Components.

Left: 1972 Elan Sprint

Above: 1971 Elan +2   *Below: 1971 Europa*

The company became profitable again after a sticky period and over 4,500 cars were produced in 1969 plus about 3,000 7s, most of which were sold as kits.

The company began producing upmarket sports cars in 1974 and the public was offered the new Elite and, later, the front-engined Eclat. The stylish mid-engined Esprit was launched in 1976, first with a normally aspirated engine, and later with a turbocharged unit that could propel this tractable road car to 160mph

(257 km/h). Lotus also supplied slant-four engines for the Jensen-Healey between 1972 and 1976.

Top right: 1962 Type 25
Right: 1967 Lotus 49 V8, 2993cc
Below right: 1969 Lotus 63 V8
Bottom right: 1970 Type 72 Formula 1

Below: 1974 Elite 2+2

Lotus Excel. Based on the Eclat model, the Excel was introduced in October 1982 with 2+2 fastback styling and powered by a 2172cc dohc four-cylinder front-mounted engine with a five-speed gearbox and rear-wheel drive.

Above: Lotus Eclat, launched 1975

Below: Esprit turbo, launched 1980

Below: Lotus Esprit, launched in 1975 with GRP body, 1973cc four-cylinder mid-mounted engine and disc brakes all round. The S2 was introduced in 1978, the 2174cc Turbo in 1980, the S3 in 1981, the Turbo HC in 1986, and a restyled version in 1987.

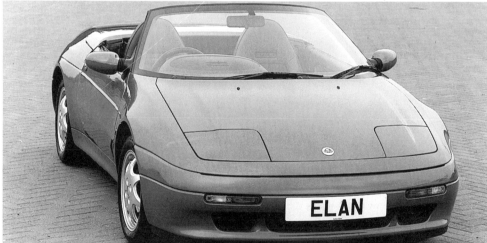

Colin Chapman died of a heart attack in December 1982 and the following year British Car Auctions bought part of the company, which was again near bankruptcy. Group Lotus was acquired by General Motors late in 1985.

Today, it continues with its own identity, producing cars such as the Excel, the all-new Elan, Esprit and stunning Esprit Turbo and conducting research into exciting new areas of vehicle design such as computer-controlled active suspension systems.

Left: 1990 Lotus Elan SE
Below: 1984 JPS Lotus 95T Formula One race car

The 1990s turned out to be an important decade for Lotus. Following a failed management buyout attempt early in the decade, the Hethel-based company, was bought in 1993 by the mysteriously wealthy Bugatti Automobili, whose chairman Romano Artioli, sold Lotuses in Italy. The company also took 200 or so unbuilt Elans, which it started to assemble and sell as the Elan S2.

Following the collapse of the Bugatti empire, Lotus was again rescued, this time by Malaysian company Proton, in 1996.

The Esprit was continually developed, or at least repackaged to keep with the times, but was perhaps the company's greatest car since the original Elan was launched in 1996.

The Elise used a 1.8-litre K-series Rover engine as used in the MGF. As in the MG it was also mid-mounted, but there the similarity ended. As with any new Lotus, it had to set new levels of handling and

Above: 1996 Lotus Elise

Below: 1997 Lotus Esprit GT3

roadholding – a job it did admirably.

With its unconventional bonded alloy chassis and finely-tuned suspension, it was praised the world over by the motoring press and was often described as the finest-handling car in the world. Despite the fact that it used only the 120bhp MGF 1.8i unit it was considerably faster than even the 143bhp MGF, due largely to its impressively light weight.

The Esprit had carried on with four-cylinder engines since its launch. It wasn't until 1997 that Lotus built its own new engine, the first since the 1970s. The new 3.5-litre V8 had a flat-plane crankshaft, common in racing engines, but almost unique in a road car. Twin turbos boosted the maximum power output to 354bhp, more than 100bhp more than the most powerful four-cylinder unit. The only drawback to the engine was that its unusual crankshaft made it sound like two four-cylinder units rather than a sporty, burbling V8. It gave the Esprit extra life to take it comfortably into the next century.

Rumours soon followed of a V8-engined Elise coupé. A car meeting this description, called the GT1, entered Le Mans in 1997.

Above right: The Lotus Esprit Sport 300 was top of the Esprit tree before the V8 arrived and was launched at the 1992 Birmingham Motor Show

Right: The GT1 used the Esprit's V8 engine in an Elise-style carbonfibre body. It competed in the Le Mans 24 Hours in 1997 but dropped out before the end

Left and below: The Esprit V8 was launched in 1996 at the Geneva Motor Show. The V8 with flat-plane crankshaft and twin turbos was Lotus' first new in-house engine since the 1970s. Power output was over 350bhp at 6,500rpm, giving a top speed of over 170mph (274km/h) and a 0-60mph (0-100km/h) time of under 4.5 seconds

Marcos

Great Britain 1959 to date

Jem Marsh and Frank Costin were the men behind Marcos and the marque was derived from their surnames.

Marsh worked in Firestone's technical department while Costin had a technical career in the aviation industry.

In 1959 Marsh founded Speedex Castings and Accessories Ltd. in Luton, Bedfordshire, to supply glassfibre shells and mechanical components to specials builders.

Costin used his knowledge of aerodynamics and skill of working with plywood to design a lightweight, high-performance two-seater car with integral body and marine ply chassis.

It had Triumph Herald front suspension and Nash Metropolitan rear.

The car was built by Marsh, who raced it successfully, and it was soon available to customers as a Marcos.

Marcos Cars Ltd. was formed in 1962 to sell the cars as kits and the following year the company moved to Bradford-on-Avon, Wiltshire.

The Marcos G.T. went on sale in 1964 with a Volvo 1800 engine, quickly followed by the 1600 G.T. with a 1.6-litre Ford engine.

The popular coupé was available later with the two-litre V4 Ford engine and the three-litre V6, eventually with a steel chassis.

The company began moving to larger premises in Westbury, Wiltshire, in 1970, and produced the four-seater Mantis. This was not a great success and only 32 were made.

Production stopped in 1972, along with the G.T., a year after the company had been sold to racing-team proprietor Rob Walker.

However, Marcos continued to build the Mini-Marcos – launched in 1965 – which used B.M.C. Mini mechanical components.

The Mini-Marcos was taken over in 1975 by D. and H. Fibreglass Techniques Ltd., of Oldham, Lancashire, and revised to become the Midas in 1978.

The company became Midas Cars and moved to Corby, Northamptonshire, in 1981 and the Metro-based Midas Gold was launched in July 1985. A fire in March 1989 destroyed Midas's production facilities, and consequent cash-flow difficulties led the company into liquid-ation – but hopeful of a buyer – by the end of the year.

Jem Marsh formed Jem Marsh Performance Cars at the old works in Westbury and put the Marcos G.T. back into production in 1981. By 1986 production was running at about two a week.

The latest models use Ford engines and, in the Marcos Mantula, the 3.5-litre Rover V8 unit.

Above right: 1960 Marcos GT
Right: Spyder convertibles and coupé

Top and above: The Mantula Spyder V8

Below: 1969 3-litre Marcos with V6 Ford power unit. The glassfibre body was mounted on a wood chassis. This lightweight low-slung 125bhp sports car could top 193km/h (125mph).

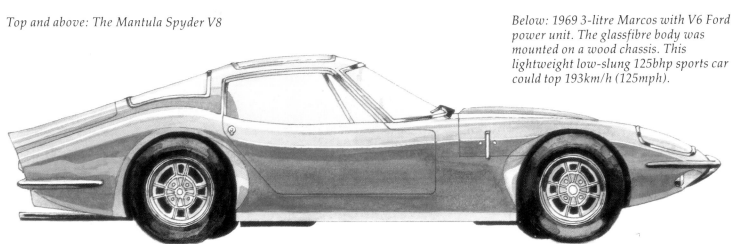

Marmon

U.S.A.
1902–1933

Howard Carpenter Marmon began producing vehicles from the family milling-machinery firm Nordyke and Marmon Co. in Indianapolis. His first car was an advanced air-cooled vee-twin developed over four years to 1902. This was not offered for sale, Marmon working instead on a four-cylinder version which appeared two years later.

Marmon stuck with V4 engines until 1908, when he went over to in-line units for ease of quantity manufacture, although he had experimented with a V6 and showed a very expensive but unsuccessful V8 at the New York Motor Show. By 1910 the Model 32 was in production, its slow start suddenly boosted by Ray Harroun's victory in the first Indianapolis 500 the following year, during Marmon's most successful competition period.

This was followed by the Model 34 in 1916, the work of two men who joined Marmon three years earlier, Frederick E. Moskovics and Alanson P. Brush. This vehicle was mainly constructed from aluminium until the outbreak of World

Above: 1911 Marmon six-cylinder
Left: 1920 Marmon Phaeton
Below: 1921 Model 34 Tourer

War I, but reappeared in 1919 with a cast-iron engine and higher price tag, although this was cut back in the early 1920s.

By 1924 the company's fortunes were failing and George M. Williams was taken on to reverse the trend, which he did by concentrating on low-cost closed models. The Marmon Motor Co. was set up in

1926, separate from the parent company, but the change in direction caused Howard Marmon to opt for semi-retirement and Barney Roos took over. Sales increased.

The Roosevelt range, offered separately from Marmon until 1930, did well until the onset of the Depression. In 1931 Howard Marmon returned plans for the Sixteen, a luxury Cadillac rival designed by Walter Darwin Teague Jr., but production delays proved fatal. In 1933 Howard Marmon personally financed a Teague-styled advanced two-door sedan design, but this failed to get off the ground. Marmon called in the receivers and the company was taken over by the American Automotive Corporation that year.

Above left: 1929 Marmon Roosevelt 3.3
Above: 1930 Marmon straight eight
Below: 1931 Marmon V16

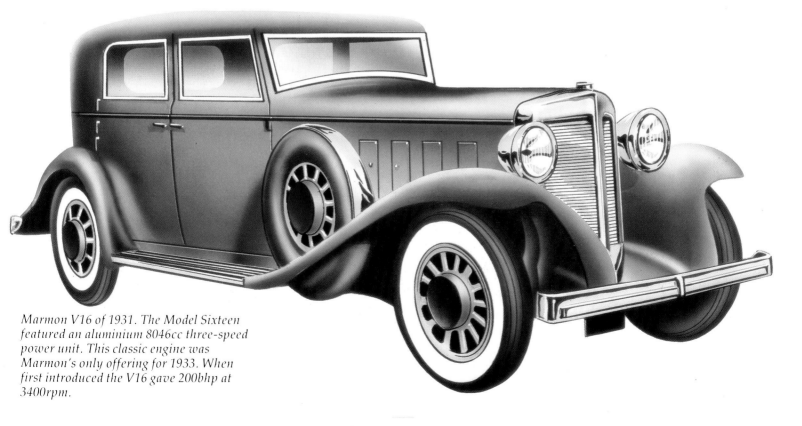

Marmon V16 of 1931. The Model Sixteen featured an aluminium 8046cc three-speed power unit. This classic engine was Marmon's only offering for 1933. When first introduced the V16 gave 200bhp at 3400rpm.

Maserati

Italy
1926 to date

The name Maserati conjures up the same image as that evoked by Ferrari. Thoroughbred motoring in the true tradition of Italian exotica.

Though never quite in the same league as Ferrari, Maserati has nevertheless been instrumental in giving Italy its reputation for high-performance four-wheeled stallions, race-track success and motoring exclusivity.

Taking their Trident motif from the statue of Neptune in Bologna, Maserati brothers Alfieri, Bindo, Ettore, Ernesto and Mario were involved in racing cars and motor-cycles and started production of their own 1.5-litre cars in 1926, the year Alfieri had a class win in the Targa Florio.

Alfieri had been undertaking development of a racing car for Diatto of Turin. When Diatto closed down, spark plug manufacturer Alfieri of Bologna took over the straight-eight design.

The family built up a reputation for racing machinery including a V16, and in the 1930s began to look more seriously at road cars, though making very few.

Above: Nuvolari in 1934 8CM3000

Above: 1938 Maserati 8CTF

Below: 1947 1500cc A6 Spyder

Below: 1925 Diatto Tipo 20. The Maserati brothers built this 2-litre Grand Prix for Diatto of Turin before setting up in business for themselves. Sleeving the Diatto down to 1.5 litres, they won the 1926 Targa Florio.

Above: 1953/4 250F straight six Grand Prix car

In 1932 Alfieri died following a racing accident. A sixth brother, Carlo, had died in 1910, so Bindo, Ettore and Ernesto carried on the business, Mario having chosen art as his career. A seventh brother died as a child..

In 1937 industrialist Adolfo Orsi purchased a controlling interest in the company which moved to Modena the following year. By 1947 it had revealed its first true (though limited) production road car, the A6-1500 with bodywork by Pininfarina.

The brothers Maserati had signed a ten-year consultancy contract with Orsi and when this expired they decided to leave, returning to Bologna to found OSCA sports cars.

Orsi and his son Omer found a winning talent in the shape of Gioacchino Colombo who had worked with Alfa Romeo and Ferrari. Colombo helped design the Maserati 250F in 1953. This Formula One car was regarded as one of the finest racing machines of the 1950s. Many famous drivers including Stirling Moss, Mike Hawthorn and Juan Fangio enjoyed considerable success with it, Fangio winning the 1957 world title in one.

That year sealed Fangio's fifth world title (and saw the introduction of the 3500GT, an indication that Maserati was growing more serious about road cars), but many Maserati drivers were involved in serious accidents and the factory was experiencing financial troubles. So the company decided to withdraw from racing

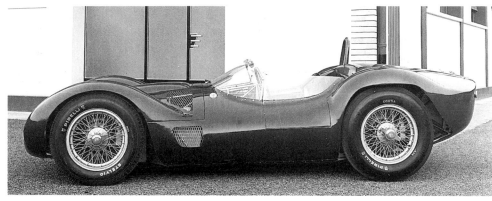

Top: 1954 A6G Allemano

Above: 1956 twin cam 250F F1 racer

Above: 1959 2000cc 'Birdcage' Tipo 60

Above: 1960s 3500GT, first seen 1957

Above: 1964 Quattro Porte

Above: Mistral Coupé

and concentrate on high-performance road cars.

It found that it could not totally divorce the name from racing, however, and won the 1960 and 1961 Nürburgring 1000km race with the Maserati 'Birdcage', so called because the chassis frame was made of many lengths of small-diameter tube.

The Maserati V12 three-litre engine also powered Cooper to Grands Prix wins in 1966 and 1967.

In 1969 Orsi sold control of Maserati to Citroën of France. Citroën wanted an engine development company to work on its SM project. The result was an extremely sophisticated car with a V6 Maserati power unit.

Orsi relinquished all interest in 1971 after an argument with Citroën over policy.

In the mid-1970s luxury-car manufacturers were going through a lean time and sales of the SM were way below expectations. Citroën tried to find a buyer for Maserati, but no one was interested, so in May 1975 it was announced that the Modena factory would have to be put into voluntary liquidation.

This announcement was designed to force some interest. The result was that the company was taken over by Alejandro de Tomaso and the Italian government agency GEPI as major stockholder.

Above: 1966 Quattro Porte   *Below: 1966 Mexico V8*

Right: 1966/7 Maserati 300S
Below right: 1966 V8 Ghibli

Left: The 8C-1100 of 1931 won its class in the Mille Miglia in 1931 and 1932. Its 1078cc engine had a Roots supercharger providing a maximum speed of 185km/h (115mph).

Above: 1970 Ghibli Spyder Ghia
Right: 1968 4.7 Ghibli Spyder

Above: 1969 V8 Indy
Left: 1971 V8 Bora
*Below: 1972 line-up. From left: Bora,
Indy, Ghibli, Mexico*

De Tomaso was put in charge of running the factory and for 1976 Aurelio Bertocchi was appointed general manager. Ing. (engineer) Casarini as head of design and Omer Orsi later rejoined as commercial director, but only until 1977 when he resigned.

In 1982 Maserati produced a profit, and students of the marque argue that this was probably the first time in Maserati history it had done so. That year the company produced 2,265 cars, almost five times the previous year's production, but by 1990 its future as an independent car maker looked increasingly uncertain.

Above: 1971 Maserati Bora
Right: 1980 V8 Kyalami Coupé
Far right top: 1972 V6 Citroën Maserati
Far right bottom: 1980 V8 Khamsin 2+2

Below: 1974 Maserati Merak SS with mid-mounted V6 of 2965cc. This compact cracker was dropped in 1984 when the range was 'rationalized'. Before then a 1999cc version was available. The Merak was first seen at the 1972 Paris Salon.

*Above: Convertible version of the 1982
1996cc V6 Biturbo (twin turbo) giving
180bhp. Hardly striking, it has been a sales
success. As a follow-up Maserati unveiled
the Biturbo 430 four-door saloon with a
250bhp 2.8-litre V6 capable of 240km/h
(150mph) in 1989.*

Right: Front-engined Biturbo
Far right: 1989 2.5 Spyder Biturbo
Below: 2-litre Biturbo Coupé

Somehow, Maserati struggled on into the 1990s and was eventually rescued by the Fiat group. Fiat bought the company in 1993 when Alejandro De Tomaso was forced to sell his 51 per cent due to illness. By then, the existing range was looking very dated.

The first model to be modernized was the Biturbo. Reborn as the Ghibli, it remained essentially the same under the skin, but the body was all new, with much fresher styling and the build quality was greatly improved.

A new Quattroporte soon followed, the famous name being revived in a stylish new four-door saloon with the same V6 engine as the Ghibli. A new 4.2-litre V8 model followed in 1995.

Left: The Maserati Biturbo convertible was beginning to look dated by the 1990s

Below: The 1997 Maserati Ghibli Cup. Sharp styling, improved build quality, and a powerful engine helped increase sales of the new two-door Maserati coupé

Index

Encyclopedai of cars   629.222
    Volume 4

MY 23 '98

JE 2 '98

JY 7 '98

JUL 29 '98

NO 9 '98

OC 0 4 07

DE 17 10

SE 0 3 13